A series of

Guidelines taken from

Sūrah Al-Fātihah

Shaykh ʿAbdur-Razzāq Ibn ʿAbdul-Muhsin al-ʿAbbād al-Badr

@ Maktabatulirshad Publications Ltd, USA

ISBN: 978-1-6494-5529-1

First Edition: Shawwāl 1441 A.H. / June 2020 C.E.

Cover Design: Muḥammad Arfaz

Translation: ʿAbdullāh Ali as-Somali

Revision & Editing: Maktabatulirshad Staff

Typesetting & Formatting: Abū Sulaymān Muḥammad ʿAbdul-Azīm ibn Joshua Baker

Subject: Tafsīr/ ʿAqīdah/ *Qur'ān*

Website: www.maktabatulirshad.com

Email: info@maktabatulirshad.com

مكتبة الإرشاد
Maktabatul-Irshad
PUBLICATIONS

TABLE OF CONTENTS

BRIEF BIOGRAPHY OF THE AUTHOR 4

TRANSLITERATION TABLE 6

INTRODUCTION 8

1ST GUIDELINE: CURING WITH *AL-FĀTIHAH* 16

2ND GUIDELINE: TAWHĪD & ITS TYPES 25

3RD GUIDELINE: SINCERITY & COMPLIANCE WITH THE SUNNAH.. 41

4TH GUIDELINE: THE STRAIGHT PATH.............................. 49

5TH GUIDELINE: A WARNING AGAINST DEVIATING FROM THE PATH OF ALLĀH... 78

6TH GUIDELINE: THE ESTABLISHMENT OF IMAAN (FAITH) IN THE LAST DAY 101

7TH GUIDELINE: ESTABLISHMENT OF THE BELIEF IN *AL-QADAR* (DIVINE PRE-DECREE 138

8TH GUIDELINE: CLARIFICATION OF THE STATUS OF DUAA (SUPPLICATION).. 173

9TH GUIDELINE: LOVE, HOPE, & FEAR.............................. 213

BRIEF BIOGRAPHY OF THE AUTHOR

His name: Shaykh ʿAbdur-Razzāq Ibn ʿAbdul-Muhsin al-ʿAbbād al-Badr who is the son of the *Allāmah* & *Muhaddith* of *Madinah*, Shaykh ʿAbdul-Muhsin al-ʿAbbād al-Badr.

Birth: He was born on the 22nd day of *Dhul-Qaʾdah* in the year 1382 A.H. in *az-Zalʾfi*, Kingdom of Saudi Arabia. He currently resides in *Madinah*.

Current Occupation: He is a member of the teaching staff at the Islāmic University of *Madinah*.

Scholarly Certifications: Doctorate in ʿAqīdah.

The Shaykh has authored books, papers of research, as well as numerous explanations in different disciplines. Among them are:

1. *Fiqh of Supplications & Legislative Remembrance.*
2. *Hajj & Refinement of Souls*
3. Explanation of the book, *Exemplary Principles'* by Shaykh Muḥammad ibn Ṣāliḥ al-ʿUthaymīn (رَحِمَهُ ٱللَّهُ).
4. Explanation of the book, *'the Principles of Names & Attributes'* authored by Shaykh ul-Islām ibn al-Qayyim (رَحِمَهُ ٱللَّهُ).
5. Explanation of the book, *'Good Words,'* authored by Shaykh ul-Islām ibn al-Qayyim (رَحِمَهُ ٱللَّهُ).
6. Explanation of the book, *'al-ʿAqīdah Tahaawiyyah.*
7. Explanation of the book, *'al-Fusūl: Biography of the Messenger'* by ibn Kathīr (رَحِمَهُ ٱللَّهُ).

8. Explanation of the book, *'al-Abab al-Mufrad*, by Imām al-Bukhārī (رَحِمَهُ ٱللَّهُ).

He studied knowledge under several scholars. The most distinguished of them are:

1. His father the *Allāmah* Shaykh ʿAbdul-Muhsin al-ʿAbbād al-Badr (حَفِظَهُ اللهُ).

2. The *Allāmah* Shaykh ʿAbdul-Azeez bin ʿAbdullāh bin Bāz (رَحِمَهُ ٱللَّهُ).

3. The *Allāmah* Shaykh Muḥammad ibn Ṣāliḥ al-ʿUthaymīn (رَحِمَهُ ٱللَّهُ).

4. Shaykh ʿAli ibn Nāsir al-Faqīhī (حَفِظَهُ اللهُ).

TRANSLITERATION TABLE

Consonants

ء	ʾ	د	d	ض	ḍ	ك	k
ب	b	ذ	dh	ط	ṭ	ل	l
ت	t	ر	r	ظ	ẓ	م	m
ث	th	ز	z	ع	ʿ	ن	n
ج	j	س	s	غ	gh	هـ	h
ح	ḥ	ش	sh	ف	f	و	w
خ	kh	ص	ṣ	ق	q	ي	y

Vowels

Short	␣َ	a	␣ِ	i	␣ُ	u
Long	␣ـَا	ā	␣ِي	ī	␣ُو	ū

Diphthongs	␣َوْ	aw	␣َيْ	ay

Arabic Symbols & their meanings

عَزَّوَجَلَّ
(Allāh) the Mighty
& Sublime

سُبْحَانَهُوَتَعَالَى
Glorified &
Exalted is Allāh

رَحِمَهُٱللَّهُ
May Allāh have
mercy on him

حَفِظَهُ اللهُ
May Allāh
preserve him

صَلَّىٱللَّهُعَلَيْهِوَعَلَىٰٓآلِهِوَسَلَّمَ
May Allāh elevate
his rank & grant
him peace

جَلَّجَلَالُهُ
(Allāh) His
Majesty is
Exalted

جَلَّوَعَلَا
(Allāh) the
Sublime &
Exalted

تَبَارَكَوَتَعَالَى
(Allāh) the
Blessed &
Exalted

رَضِيَٱللَّهُعَنْهُمْ
May Allāh be
pleased with them

رَضِيَٱللَّهُعَنْهَا
May Allāh be
pleased with her

رَضِيَٱللَّهُعَنْهُ
May Allāh be
pleased with
him

عَلَيْهِٱلصَّلَاةُوَٱلسَّلَامُ
May Allāh
elevate his rank
& grant him
peace

رَحِمَهُمُٱللَّهُ
May Allāh have
mercy upon them

INTRODUCTION

All praise and thanks are due to Allāh; we praise Him, seek His Help, and we seek His Forgiveness. We seek refuge with Him from the evil of our souls and the evil of our actions. Whosoever Allāh guides, then none can misguide him, and whosoever Allāh leaves to go stray, then none can guide him. I bear witness that there is none worthy of worship except Allāh, the One Who has no partner. I bear witness that Muḥammad is His servant and Messenger, may Allāh raise his rank and send peace and blessings upon him, his family and companions.

Indeed, *Sūrah al-Fātihah* is an excellent chapter from the chapters of the *Qur'ān*. We are obligated to read it seventeen times daily in the five mandatory prayers as it must be recited in every unit of the *Salāh* (prayer). It has been affirmed in the authentic *Hadīth* of the Prophet—صَلَّى ٱللَّهُ عَلَيْهِ وَسَلَّمَ—that he said:

لَا صَلَاةَ لِمَنْ لَمْ يَقْرَأْ بِفَاتِحَةِ الْكِتَابِ

"There is no prayer for the one who does not recite the *Fātihah* of the Book."[1]

Furthermore, he said in the other *Hadīth*:

---

[1] Reported by al-Bukhārī (756) and Muslim (395)

مَنْ صَلَّى صَلَاةً لَمْ يَقْرَأْ فِيهَا بِأُمِّ الْقُرْآنِ فَهِيَ خِدَاجٌ

"Whoever prays a *Salāh* without having recited Umm al-Qur'ān, then it (his *Salāh*) is *Khidā*, '"[2] meaning, it is unfinished.

When the servant performs his *Rawātib*[3] and extra voluntary prayers, his recitation of *al-Fātihah* throughout the day & night will become more frequent. In the same fashion his recitation of *al-Fātihah* throughout the months and years will increase significantly. *Sūrah al-Fātihah* is the best chapter of the *Qur'ān* as has been affirmed by the noble Messenger (صَلَّىٰاللَّهُعَلَيْهِوَسَلَّمَ).

On the authority of Abū Sa'īd al-Mu'alimī—ﷺ—who said:

كُنْتُ أُصَلِّي فِي الْمَسْجِدِ فَدَعَانِي رَسُولُ اللَّهِ صلى الله عليه وسلم فَلَمْ أُجِبْهُ، فَقُلْتُ يَا رَسُولَ اللَّهِ إِنِّي كُنْتُ أُصَلِّي. فَقَالَ " أَلَمْ يَقُلِ اللَّهُ (اسْتَجِيبُوا لِلَّهِ وَلِلرَّسُولِ إِذَا دَعَاكُمْ) ثُمَّ قَالَ لِي لأُعَلِّمَنَّكَ سُورَةً هِيَ أَعْظَمُ السُّوَرِ فِي الْقُرْآنِ قَبْلَ أَنْ تَخْرُجَ مِنَ الْمَسْجِدِ ". ثُمَّ أَخَذَ بِيَدِي، فَلَمَّا أَرَادَ أَنْ يَخْرُجَ قُلْتُ لَهُ أَلَمْ تَقُلْ " لأُعَلِّمَنَّكَ سُورَةً هِيَ أَعْظَمُ سُورَةٍ

---

[2] Reported by Muslim (395)
[3] **TN:** the optional units of prayers offered after specific obligatory *Salāh*.

فِي الْقُرْآنِ ". قَالَ " (الْحَمْدُ لِلَّهِ رَبِّ الْعَالَمِينَ) هِيَ السَّبْعُ الْمَثَانِي وَالْقُرْآنُ الْعَظِيمُ الَّذِي أُوتِيتُهُ

"I was praying in the Masjid when the Messenger of Allāh (ﷺ) called me, but I did not answer him. I said: 'O Allāh's Messenger (ﷺ), I was praying.' He said: 'Did Allāh not say: 'Give your response to Allāh (by obeying Him) and to His Apostle when he calls you?' (8:24) He then said to me, 'I will teach you a *Sūrah* which is the greatest *Sūrah* in the *Qur'ān* before you leave the Masjid.' Then he got hold of my hand, and when he intended to leave the Masjid, I said to him, 'Didn't you say to me, 'I will teach you a *Sūrah* which is the greatest *Sūrah* in the *Qur'ān*?' He said: '*Al-Hamdu-Lil-lāh Rabbi-l-ʿĀlamīn*, (Praise be to Allāh, the Lord of the worlds), which is *as-Sab' al- Mathānī* (the seven repeatedly recited Verses) and the Grand *Qur'ān* which has been given to me.'"[4]

So if it was a must from the one performing *Salāh* to answer the Messenger (ﷺ) when he calls, then how about the one who is busy with the worldly-life or with trivial matters, then the order to perform the *Salāh* (in its proper time) comes to him, and he does not answer?

---

[4] Reported by al-Bukhārī (4474)

This blessed *Sūrah* has many names that indicate the greatness of its status and value; it is called:

❖ *Fātihatul-Kitāb* (The Opening Chapter of the Book); because when you open the *Qur'ān*, the first chapter that you will find is *al-Fātihah*—it is the first *Sūrah* of the *Qur'ān*.

❖ *as-Sab' al-Mathānī*[5]: It is called '*as-Sab'* because its verses are seven and '*al-Mathāni*' because it is repeated in every *Salāh*. You recite it in every unit of every prayer—and this is from the qualities that are specific to *Sūrah al-Fātihah*.

❖ *al-Qur'ān al-'Aẓīm* (The Grand *Qur'ān*): The Prophet (ﷺ) named it this even though it is only a single chapter from the chapters of the *Qur'ān*; this is because it covers what is included in the entirety of the *Qur'ān*. So, all of the knowledge in the *Qur'ān* from *Tawhīd* (singling out Allāh alone in worship), commandments, prohibitions, stories, and tales is summarized in *Sūrah al-Fātihah* and mentioned in detail in the Noble *Qur'ān*.

This *Sūrah* is a tremendous light and an illuminating beam that Allāh has honored his Prophet Muḥammad (ﷺ) and his nation with. On the authority of Ibn 'Abbās (رضي الله عنه) who said:

---

[5] **TN:** The Seven oft-repeated Verses.

بَيْنَمَا جِبْرِيلُ قَاعِدٌ عِنْدَ النَّبِيِّ صلى الله عليه وسلم سَمِعَ نَقِيضًا مِنْ

فَوْقِهِ فَرَفَعَ رَأْسَهُ فَقَالَ هَذَا بَابٌ مِنَ السَّمَاءِ فُتِحَ الْيَوْمَ لَمْ يُفْتَحْ قَطُّ إِلاَّ

الْيَوْمَ فَنَزَلَ مِنْهُ مَلَكٌ فَقَالَ هَذَا مَلَكٌ نَزَلَ إِلَى الأَرْضِ لَمْ يَنْزِلْ قَطُّ إِلاَّ

الْيَوْمَ فَسَلَّمَ وَقَالَ أَبْشِرْ بِنُورَيْنِ أُوتِيتَهُمَا لَمْ يُؤْتَهُمَا نَبِيٌّ قَبْلَكَ فَاتِحَةُ

الْكِتَابِ وَخَوَاتِيمُ سُورَةِ الْبَقَرَةِ لَنْ تَقْرَأَ بِحَرْفٍ مِنْهُمَا إِلاَّ أُعْطِيتَهُ

"While Jibrīl (Gabriel) was sitting with the Messenger of Allāh (ﷺ), he heard a sound above him. He lifted his head, and said: 'This is a gate which has been opened in heaven today. It was never opened before.' Then an angel descended through it, he said: 'This is an angel who has come down to earth. He never came down before.' He sent greetings and said: 'Rejoice with two lights given to you. Such lights were not given to any Prophet before you. These (lights) are: Fātihatul-Kitāb (*Surah al-Fātihah*), and the concluding verses of *Surah* al-Baqarah. You will never recite a word from them without being given the blessings it contains.'"[6]

So, according to what the angel said in the *Hadīth*, al-Fātihah is from the matters that are specific to the noble Prophet (عَلَيْهِ ٱلصَّلَاةُ وَٱلسَّلَامُ) and his nation: "Such lights were not given to any Prophet before you." This is from the favor of Allāh upon the nation of Islām—an

---

[6] Reported by Muslim (806)

angel came down carrying this glad tiding even though it was Jibrīl (عَلَيْهِٱلسَّلَامُ) who descended with its revelation before that:

"And truly, this (the *Qur'ān*) is a revelation from the Lord of the *'Ālamīn* (mankind, jinn and all that exists), (192) Which the trustworthy *Rūh* [Jibrīl (Gabriel)] has brought down." [Sūrah ash-Shu'arā (26):192-193]

Descent with the *Qur'ān* was from the specific qualities of Jibrīl (عَلَيْهِٱلسَّلَامُ). This angel came as a bringer of good news to the Prophet (عَلَيْهِٱلصَّلَاةُوَٱلسَّلَامُ) and his nation following Jibrīl due to the virtues of this *Sūrah*—from which is that the servant will be rewarded multiplied good deeds and abundant rewards by Allāh (سُبْحَانَهُوَتَعَالَى) according to the number of its letters whenever he recites it. So, we thank Allāh (عَزَّوَجَلَّ) for favoring us with the recitation of this *Sūrah*. And thanking Allāh (عَزَّوَجَلَّ) for this blessing entails that this *Sūrah* is given its due right from reciting it correctly, soundly understanding it, and fulfilling what it requires from piety, steadfastness and treading the Straight Path of Allāh; and that his only portion from the *Sūrah* is not a mere recitation of its words, rather it has to be a recitation encompassing the three types of *Tilāwah:* Allāh (سُبْحَانَهُوَتَعَالَى) said:

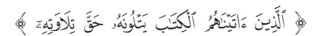

"Those (who embraced Islām from Banī Israel) to whom We gave the Book [the Torah] [or those (Muḥammad's (ﷺ) Companions) to whom We have given the Book (the *Qur'ān*)] recite it (i.e., obey its orders and follow its teachings) as it should be recited (i.e., followed)." [Sūrah al-Baqarah (2):121]

It is said that: "*Talā Fulān Fulānan*" (So and so followed so and so). So, the word *Talā* (which comes from *Tilāwah*) [also] means to follow. Thus, the *Tilāwah* of this *Sūrah* encompasses: reciting it and sounding its letters correctly, following its understandings and comprehending its meanings, and fulfilling what it contains from adhering to the Straight Path of Allāh and remaining steadfast on the right path which will guide the servant to happiness in this life and the Hereafter.

Therefore, whoever merely recites the letters of this *Sūrah* or any other one from the *Qur'ān* (i.e., without understanding and following its teachings), then he has not truly recited the *Qur'ān* and followed it. Rather, he must also establish its boundaries by fulfilling its commands and abstaining from its prohibitions.

Allāh (سُبْحَانَهُوَتَعَالَى) revealed the *Qur'ān* so that its verses could be pondered over and acted upon:

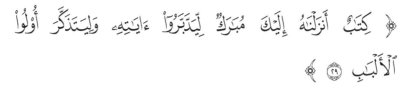

"(This is) a Book (the *Qur'ān*) which We have sent down to you, full of blessings that they may ponder over its

Verses, and that men of understanding may remember."
[Sūrah Sād (38):29]

So if we need pondering and reflecting over the *Qur'ān* and understanding it, then our need for due contemplation over *al-Fātihah*—which is the Mother of The *Qur'ān*, the best chapter in the *Qur'ān* and the one generally containing what the entirety of the *Qur'ān* covers —is more dire and severe. This is why it behooves every believing servant to give this magnificent *Sūrah* what it deserves from the contemplation and understanding of its meanings and proofs so that he can benefit and ascend by the grace of the King and the Giver of All (Allāh).

This book contains a reference to some of the guidelines of this blessed *Sūrah,* along with its tremendous benefits and abundant goodness—the origin of which are lessons that I gave and then later revised, summarized, and released in this form. I hope that Allāh brings about religious and worldly gains and benefits through it. I firstly and lastly praise Allāh, and I thank Him inwardly and outwardly. I cannot let this moment pass to extend my gratitude to my brother, the virtuous Shaykh, 'Abdul-Hādī Ibn Hasan Wahabī, for his appreciated efforts and noble work to produce this book. May Allāh reward him with good and place this (his endeavors) on his scale of good deed.

I ask Allāh, the Most Generous for *Tawfīq* (ability to be successful) and acceptance. May He elevate the rank of our Prophet Muḥammad and send peace upon him, his family, and companions.

1ˢᵀ GUIDELINE: CURING WITH *AL-FĀTIHAH*

From the names of *Sūrah al-Fātihah* is '*al-Kāfiyah ash-Shāfiyah*' (The Sufficient Curer). It contains a cure for the diseases of the heart and the body. If there is a corrupted desire or intention, or *Riyā* (desire for performing deeds to show off), arrogance, oppression, and transgression or other than that in the heart, then its cure is in *ash-Shāfiyah* (i.e., *Sūrah al-Fātihah*)

Ibn al-Qayyim (رَحِمَهُٱللَّهُ) says: I use to frequently hear Ibn Taymiyyah say: "**You Alone we worship**" (1:5) contains a cure for *Riyā* (showing off) and "**and You Alone we seek assistance from**" (1:5) includes a treatment for arrogance.

So "**You Alone we worship,**" (1:5) removes the disease of showing off and pretending for the creation while reminding the servant of the station of *Ikhlās* (sincerity in worship)—which is from the noblest of stations—and the greatness of the reward of its people as Allāh (سُبْحَانَهُوَتَعَالَى) says:

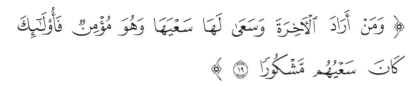

﴿ وَمَنْ أَرَادَ ٱلْآخِرَةَ وَسَعَىٰ لَهَا سَعْيَهَا وَهُوَ مُؤْمِنٌ فَأُوْلَٰئِكَ كَانَ سَعْيُهُم مَّشْكُورًا ۝ ﴾

"And whoever desires the Hereafter and strives for it, with the necessary effort due (i.e., righteous deeds of Allāh's Obedience) while he is a believer (in the Oneness of Allāh— Islāmic Monotheism), then such are the ones whose striving shall be appreciated, (thanked and rewarded by Allāh)." [Sūrah al-Isrā (17):19]

And **"and You Alone we seek assistance from,"** (1:5) acquaints the servant with his dire need for his Lord and his constant need of assistance from Him (سُبْحَانَهُوَتَعَالَى) as Allāh (سُبْحَانَهُوَتَعَالَى) said:

$$﴿ ۞ يَٰٓأَيُّهَا ٱلنَّاسُ أَنتُمُ ٱلۡفُقَرَآءُ إِلَى ٱللَّهِ ۖ وَٱللَّهُ هُوَ ٱلۡغَنِيُّ ٱلۡحَمِيدُ ۝ ﴾$$

"O mankind! It is you who need Allāh, But Allāh is Rich (Free of all needs), Worthy of all praise." [Sūrah Fātir (35):15]

Like this, the rest of the verses in *al-Fātihah* treat the illnesses of the heart—it contains a cure for what is in the breasts. And if there is any illness or disease in the rest of the body, *al-Fātihah* has a treatment for it as well.

On the authority of Abū Sa'īd (ﷺ) who said:

انْطَلَقَ نَفَرٌ مِنْ أَصْحَابِ النَّبِيِّ صلى الله عليه وسلم فِي سَفْرَةٍ سَافَرُوهَا حَتَّى نَزَلُوا عَلَى حَيٍّ مِنْ أَحْيَاءِ الْعَرَبِ فَاسْتَضَافُوهُمْ، فَأَبَوْا أَنْ يُضَيِّفُوهُمْ،

فَلُدِغَ سَيِّدُ ذَلِكَ الْحَيِّ، فَسَعَوْا لَهُ بِكُلِّ شَيْءٍ لاَ يَنْفَعُهُ شَيْءٌ، فَقَالَ بَعْضُهُمْ لَوْ أَتَيْتُمْ هَؤُلاَءِ الرَّهْطِ الَّذِينَ نَزَلُوا لَعَلَّهُ أَنْ يَكُونَ عِنْدَ بَعْضِهِمْ شَيْءٌ، فَأَتَوْهُمْ، فَقَالُوا يَا أَيُّهَا الرَّهْطُ، إِنَّ سَيِّدَنَا لُدِغَ، وَسَعَيْنَا لَهُ بِكُلِّ شَيْءٍ لاَ يَنْفَعُهُ، فَهَلْ عِنْدَ أَحَدٍ مِنْكُمْ مِنْ شَيْءٍ فَقَالَ بَعْضُهُمْ نَعَمْ وَاللَّهِ إِنِّي لَأَرْقِي، وَلَكِنْ وَاللَّهِ لَقَدِ اسْتَضَفْنَاكُمْ فَلَمْ تُضِيِّفُونَا، فَمَا أَنَا بِرَاقٍ لَكُمْ حَتَّى تَجْعَلُوا لَنَا جُعْلاً. فَصَالَحُوهُمْ عَلَى قَطِيعٍ مِنَ الْغَنَمِ، فَانْطَلَقَ يَتْفِلُ عَلَيْهِ وَيَقْرَأُ ﴿الْحَمْدُ لِلَّهِ رَبِّ الْعَالَمِينَ﴾ فَكَأَنَّمَا نُشِطَ مِنْ عِقَالٍ، فَانْطَلَقَ يَمْشِي وَمَا بِهِ قَلَبَةٌ، قَالَ فَأَوْفَوْهُمْ جُعْلَهُمُ الَّذِي صَالَحُوهُمْ عَلَيْهِ، فَقَالَ بَعْضُهُمُ اقْسِمُوا. فَقَالَ الَّذِي رَقَى لاَ تَفْعَلُوا، حَتَّى نَأْتِيَ النَّبِيَّ صلى الله عليه وسلم فَنَذْكُرَ لَهُ الَّذِي كَانَ، فَنَنْظُرَ مَا يَأْمُرُنَا. فَقَدِمُوا عَلَى رَسُولِ اللَّهِ صلى الله عليه وسلم فَذَكَرُوا لَهُ، فَقَالَ " وَمَا يُدْرِيكَ أَنَّهَا رُقْيَةٌ ـ ثُمَّ قَالَ ـ قَدْ أَصَبْتُمُ اقْسِمُوا وَاضْرِبُوا لِي مَعَكُمْ سَهْمًا ". فَضَحِكَ رَسُولُ اللَّهِ صلى الله عليه وسلم.

"Some of the companions of the Prophet (ﷺ) went on a journey until they reached one of the Arab tribes (at night). They asked the latter to treat them as their guests, but they refused. The chief of that tribe was then bitten by a snake (or stung by a scorpion), and they tried their best to cure him but to no avail. Some of them said: 'Will you go to the people who resided here at night, it may be that some of them might possess something (as treatment).' They went to the group of the companions (of the Prophet (ﷺ)) and said, "Our chief has been bitten by a snake (or stung by a scorpion), and we have tried everything, but he has not benefited. Have you got anything (useful)?' One of them replied, "Yes, by Allāh! I can recite *Ruqyah* (treatment with the *Qur'ān* and Prophetic supplications). Still, as you have refused to accept us as your guests, I will not recite the *Ruqyah* for you unless you fix for us some wages for it in return.' They agreed to pay them a flock of sheep. One of them then went and recited (*Sūrah al-Fātihah*): "All the praises are for the Lord of the Worlds" and puffed over the chief who became all right as if he was released from a chain, and got up and started walking, showing no signs of sickness. They paid them what they agreed to pay. Some of them (i.e., the companions) then suggested dividing their earnings among themselves. Still, the one who performed the recitation said: 'Do not divide them till we go to the Prophet (ﷺ) and narrate the whole story to him, and wait for his order.' So, they went to Allāh's Messenger (ﷺ) and narrated the story. Allāh's Messenger (ﷺ) asked: 'How did you come to know that *Sūrah al-Fātihah* is *Ruqyah*?' Then he added, 'You have done the right thing. Divide (what you have

earned) and assign a share for me as well.' The Prophet (ﷺ) smiled thereupon."[7]

Ibn al-Qayyim (رحمه الله) said in his book, *al-Jawāb al-Kāfī:* "I remained in Makkah for a period in which I fell ill with different sicknesses, and I could not find a doctor. So, I use to treat myself with *al-Fātihah,* and I would see that it had shocking effects. As a result, I began to prescribe this to anyone complaining of an ailment, and many of them would recover quickly." [8]

Using this *Sūrah* as treatment requires a recitation with certainty and confidence in Allāh (عزوجل). If unwavering certainty and trust in Allāh are both present, then the servant will reap the full benefits of such a recitation.

Going back to using this *Sūrah* for treating ailments of the heart; it is entirely known that hearts are afflicted with many types of sicknesses, and their malady is more severe than diseases of the body because the heart is the basis for all deeds and its soundness is an indication of the robustness of the body; its corruption is an indication for the depravity of the rest of the body as he (عليه الصلاة والسلام) said:

---

[7] Reported by al-Bukhārī (2276) and Muslim (2201)

[8] Look in the books: *ad-Dā wad-Dawā* and *al-Jawāb al-Kāfī* (8), 'Ālam al-Fawāid Edition. And Ibn al-Qayyim (رحمه الله) has made some statements about the effects of *Sūrah al-Fātihah* in *Zād al-Ma'ād* (4/176-178)

أَلاَ وَإِنَّ فِي الْجَسَدِ مُضْغَةً إِذَا صَلَحَتْ صَلَحَ الْجَسَدُ كُلُّهُ، وَإِذَا فَسَدَتْ

فَسَدَ الْجَسَدُ كُلُّهُ. أَلاَ وَهِيَ الْقَلْبُ

"Beware! There is a piece of flesh in the body if it becomes good (reformed), the whole body becomes good, but if it gets spoiled, the whole body gets spoiled, and that is the heart."[9]

Thus, Abū Hurairah (ﷺ) said:

الْقَلْبُ مَلِكُ الْأَعْضَاءِ جُنُودُهُ، فَإِذَا طَابَ الْمَلِكُ طَابَ الْـجُنْدُ، وَإِذَا فَسَدَ

الْمَلِكُ فَسَدَ الْـجُنْدُ. وَالْقَلْبُ كَذَلِكَ بَلْ أَشَدُّ، فَإِذَا صَلَحَ الْقَلْبُ صَلَحَ

الْبَدَنُ تَبَعاً لَهُ، وَإِذَا فَسَدَ الْقَلْبُ فَسَدَ الْبَدَنُ تَبَعاً لَهُ، فَصَلاَحُ النَّاسِ

وَاسْتِقَامَةُ أَحْوَالِهِمْ وَطِيبُ أَعْمَالِهِمْ وَسَدَادُ أَقْوَالِهِمْ رَاجِعٌ إِلَى صَلاَحِ

قُلُوبِهِمْ.

"The heart is the king, and the organs are its army. If the king is good, then the army will be good; and if the king is ruined, then the army will be ruined. And this is even truer with the heart; if the heart is rectified, the body will consequently become rectified; and if the heart becomes spoiled, then the body will consequently become spoiled.

---

[9] A segment from the *Hadīth* reported by al-Bukhārī (52) and Muslim (1599)

So, one's rectification and their states and the soundness of their deeds and statements go back to the reform of the heart."

In general, the ailments of the heart are one of two types: diseases of doubt and maladies of desires; and there is a cure for both of these two types in His (سُبْحَانَهُوَتَعَالَى) statement:

$$ ﴿ غَيْرِ ٱلْمَغْضُوبِ عَلَيْهِمْ وَلَا ٱلضَّآلِّينَ ۝ ﴾ $$

"...Not (the way) of those who earned Your Anger (such as the Jews), nor of those who went astray (such as the Christians)." [Sūrah al-Fātihah (1):7]

"**Those who earned Your anger**" had corruption in their intentions and aims, and "**those who went astray**" had depravity in their knowledge. And both of these are extremely dangerous to a person, whether the corruption is tied to one's intentions or perception and understanding. Whoever's motives become corrupt—and refuge is sought with Allāh—then he will not benefit from his knowledge and the verses of Allāh (تَبَارَكَوَتَعَالَى) which are recited to him. Thus, Allāh (جَلَّوَعَلَا) said:

$$ ﴿ مَثَلُ ٱلَّذِينَ حُمِّلُوا ٱلتَّوْرَىٰةَ ثُمَّ لَمْ يَحْمِلُوهَا كَمَثَلِ ٱلْحِمَارِ يَحْمِلُ أَسْفَارًا ﴾ $$

"The likeness of those who were entrusted with the (obligation of the) Torah (i.e., to obey its commandments

and to practice its laws), but who subsequently failed in those (obligations), is as the likeness of a donkey which carries huge burdens of books (but understands nothing from them)." [Sūrah al-Jumu'ah (62):5]

"...Who were entrusted with the (obligation of the) (Torah)," meaning it was revealed to them in their language and it was recited to them and they understood it; "...but who subsequently failed in those (obligations)," meaning they abandoned acting upon it due to the corruption in their intentions and desires and with this they earned the wrath and displeasure of Allāh. Accordingly, Allāh (سُبْحَانَهُ وَتَعَالَى) described them as being those who received the anger of Allāh; because Allāh granted them knowledge, the verses of Allāh in their language and proofs, however, they had forsaken its implementation, submitting to the order of Allāh and obeying His legislation. So, this *Sūrah* treats this disease as it directs one to seek refuge with Allāh from it.

And Allāh's (سُبْحَانَهُ وَتَعَالَى) statement: "those who went astray," (*al-Fātihah*: 7) remedies the corrupted knowledge of those who have a desire to perform good deeds and acts of worship but lack of religious understanding, yet still worship Allāh without sure knowledge and clear proofs from the Book and the Sunnah—and this is indeed misguidance from which refuge should be sought with Allāh. Therefore, if the Muslim reads this, asking Allāh for guidance to His Straight Path and that He distances him from the path of those who earned His wrath and those went astray and he frequently repeats it in the day as legislated; then this will cure the corruption of his heart—by the will of Allāh (عَزَّوَجَلَّ)—because he will continue to realize his need for the rectification of his intentions and knowledge and his dire need for remaining steadfast upon Allāh's Straight Path. So, he should endlessly and repeatedly ask his Lord (سُبْحَانَهُوَتَعَالَى) [for this]. He is—by way of this—taking the legislated means through which he will attain all good, success, and happiness in this life and the next.

Thus, this incredible, noble and blessed *Sūrah* has come to treat all the different types of ailments that can afflict the heart, reforming its defects for whomever Allāh (عَزَّوَجَلَّ) honors with the capability of effectively using it as a treatment and benefiting from it.

2ND GUIDELINE: TAWHĪD & ITS TYPES

Sūrah al-Fātihah contains the three different types of *Tawhīd* for which Allāh created us and for the sake of its implementation brought us into existence as Allāh (عَزَّوَجَلَّ) said:

$$﴿ وَمَا خَلَقْتُ ٱلْجِنَّ وَٱلْإِنسَ إِلَّا لِيَعْبُدُونِ ۝ ﴾$$

"And I (Allāh) created not the jinn and mankind except that they should worship Me (Alone)." [Sūrah adh-Dhāriyāt (51):56]

And Allāh (سُبْحَانَهُۥوَتَعَالَى) said:

$$﴿ ٱللَّهُ ٱلَّذِى خَلَقَ سَبْعَ سَمَٰوَٰتٍ وَمِنَ ٱلْأَرْضِ مِثْلَهُنَّ يَتَنَزَّلُ ٱلْأَمْرُ بَيْنَهُنَّ لِتَعْلَمُوٓا۟ أَنَّ ٱللَّهَ عَلَىٰ كُلِّ شَىْءٍ قَدِيرٌ وَأَنَّ ٱللَّهَ قَدْ أَحَاطَ بِكُلِّ شَىْءٍ عِلْمًۢا ۝ ﴾$$

"It is Allāh Who has created seven heavens and of the earth the like thereof (i.e., seven). His Command descends between them (heavens and earth) that you may know that Allāh has power over all things and that Allāh surrounds all things in (His) Knowledge." [Sūrah at-Ṭalāq (65):12]

In the first verse, He created for the purpose of worship. In the second verse, He created so we could know; therefore, we have been created for the sole servitude of Allāh and gaining knowledge about Him (سُبْحَانَهُوَتَعَالَى). For this reason, the scholars say: *Tawhīd* is two types: *Tawhīd 'Amalī* (*Tawhīd* of action) and *Tawhīd 'Ilmī* (*Tawhīd* of knowledge).

Tawhīd 'Amalī (which is *Tawhīd al-Ulūhiyyah* (to single out Allāh alone in worship)) means: To perform the *Salāh* only for Allāh, to sacrifice only for Allāh, to swear an oath only by Allāh, to invoke only Allāh, to seek aid only from Allāh and to seek support, assistance, and victory only from Allāh.

Tawhīd 'Ilmī (which is *Tawhīd al-Rubūbiyyah* (to single out Allāh in His actions) and *Tawhīd al-Asmā was-Sifāt* (to single out Allāh alone by way of His Beautiful Names and Attributes)) means: To know Allāh (سُبْحَانَهُوَتَعَالَى) and to believe in Him, His Lordship, His Sovereignty, His Splendidness, His Perfectness, His Names, and His Attributes:

﴿ هُوَ ٱللَّهُ ٱلَّذِى لَآ إِلَٰهَ إِلَّا هُوَ عَٰلِمُ ٱلْغَيْبِ وَٱلشَّهَٰدَةِ هُوَ ٱلرَّحْمَٰنُ ٱلرَّحِيمُ ۝ هُوَ ٱللَّهُ ٱلَّذِى لَآ إِلَٰهَ إِلَّا هُوَ ٱلْمَلِكُ ٱلْقُدُّوسُ ٱلسَّلَٰمُ ٱلْمُؤْمِنُ ٱلْمُهَيْمِنُ ٱلْعَزِيزُ ٱلْجَبَّارُ ٱلْمُتَكَبِّرُ سُبْحَٰنَ ٱللَّهِ عَمَّا يُشْرِكُونَ ۝ هُوَ ٱللَّهُ ٱلْخَٰلِقُ

ٱلۡبَارِئُ ٱلۡمُصَوِّرُ لَهُ ٱلۡأَسۡمَآءُ ٱلۡحُسۡنَىٰ يُسَبِّحُ لَهُۥ مَا فِى ٱلسَّمَٰوَٰتِ وَٱلۡأَرۡضِ وَهُوَ ٱلۡعَزِيزُ ٱلۡحَكِيمُ ۝

"He is Allāh, beside Whom 'Lā ilāha illā Huwa' (none has the right to be worshipped but He) the All-Knower of the unseen and the seen. He is the Most Gracious, the Most Merciful. He is Allāh beside Whom is 'Lā ilāha illā Huwa' (none has the right to be worshipped but He) the King, the Holy, the One Free from all defects, the Giver of security, the Watcher over His creatures, the All-Mighty, the Compeller, the Supreme. Glory be to Allāh! (High is He) above all that they associate as partners with Him. He is Allāh, the Creator, the Inventor of all things, the Bestower of forms. To Him belong the Best Names. All that is in the heavens and the earth glorify Him. And He is the All-Mighty, the All-Wise." [Sūrah al-Ḥashr (59):22-24]

So you [must] know that He is the Owner, the Sustainer, the One who directs (all affairs of creation) and the Disposer of all Affairs in this universe; The One who created you to worship Him Alone, to only obey and submit to Him. So do not call upon except Allāh, do not invoke except Allāh, only seek aid from Allāh and only request support and assistance from Allāh—this is *Tawhīd*, the *Tawhīd* which is the foundation of the religion, the soul of Islām and the symbol of happiness. And a person will not be able to reform himself or be purified or have his deeds accepted except with *Tawhīd*; if *Tawhīd* is missing, then the doer of the deed will not benefit from his actions or acts of worship because *Tawhīd* is the basis and the measure for the acceptance of deeds; with its presence, deeds will be sound and accepted, and in its absence, they will be void and rejected as Allāh said:

$$﴿ وَلَقَدْ أُوحِيَ إِلَيْكَ وَإِلَى ٱلَّذِينَ مِن قَبْلِكَ لَئِنْ أَشْرَكْتَ لَيَحْبَطَنَّ عَمَلُكَ وَلَتَكُونَنَّ مِنَ ٱلْخَاسِرِينَ ۝ بَلِ ٱللَّهَ فَٱعْبُدْ وَكُن مِّنَ ٱلشَّاكِرِينَ ۝ ﴾$$

"And indeed it has been revealed to you (O Muḥammad (ﷺ), as it was to those (Allāh's Messengers) before you: "If you join others in worship with Allāh, (then) surely (all) your deeds will be in vain, and you will certainly be among the losers." Nay! But worship Allāh (Alone and no one else), and be among the grateful."
[Sūrah az-Zumar (39):65-66]

And the Prophet (ﷺ) said:

$$الدُّعَاءُ هُوَ الْعِبَادَةُ$$

"*Du'aa* (calling upon and invoking Allāh) is worship."[10]

The Messenger of Allāh (ﷺ) also said to Ibn 'Abbās:

---

[10] Reported by Abū Dāwūd (1479) and authenticated by al-Albānī (رحمه الله) in *Saḥīḥ Sunan Abī Dāwūd* (1/407)

إِذَا سَأَلْت فَاسْأَلْ اللَّهَ، وَإِذَا اسْتَعَنْت فَاسْتَعِنْ بِاللَّهِ، وَاعْلَمْ أَنَّ الْأُمَّةَ لَوْ

اجْتَمَعَتْ عَلَى أَنْ يَنْفَعُوك بِشَيْءٍ لَمْ يَنْفَعُوك إِلَّا بِشَيْءٍ قَدْ كَتَبَهُ اللَّهُ

لَك، وَإِنْ اجْتَمَعُوا عَلَى أَنْ يَضُرُّوك بِشَيْءٍ لَمْ يَضُرُّوك إِلَّا بِشَيْءٍ قَدْ كَتَبَهُ

اللَّهُ عَلَيْك؛ رُفِعَتْ الْأَقْلَامُ، وَجَفَّتْ الصُّحُفُ

"If you beg, beg of Him Alone, and if you need assistance, supplicate to Allāh Alone for help. And remember that if all the people gather to benefit you, they will not be able to benefit you except with that which Allāh had foreordained (for you). If all of them gather to do harm to you, they will not be able to afflict you with anything other than that which Allāh had pre-destined against you. The pens have been lifted, and the ink has dried up."[11]

And *Sūrah al-Fātihah* provides evidence for these three types of *Tawhīd*.

As for His statement,

﴿ ٱلْحَمْدُ لِلَّهِ رَبِّ ٱلْعَٰلَمِينَ ﴾

"All the praises and thanks be to Allāh, the Lord of the ʿĀlamīn (mankind, jinn and all that exists) (1:1): *al-Hamd* is praise for

---

[11] Reported by at-Tirmidhī (2516) and authenticated by al-Albānī (رَحِمَهُٰٱللَّهُ) in *Sahīh Sunan at-Tirmidhī* (2/610)

Allāh (عَزَّوَجَلَّ), His Beautiful Names, Lofty Attributes, and His many blessings and favors—that cannot be enumerated—with love:

$$﴿ وَإِن تَعُدُّواْ نِعْمَتَ ٱللَّهِ لَا تُحْصُوهَآ ﴾$$

"And if you count the Blessings of Allāh, never could you be able to count them." [Sūrah Ibrāhīm (14):34]

Hence, His servants praise and thank Him due to His Magnificence, Excellence, and Greatness. Because He is The Bestower of Blessings, The Conferrer of Grace and Kindness, The Bestower of Various Bounties and Favors upon His servants—He (سُبْحَانَهُوَتَعَالَى) is deserving of praise and thanks and extolment. The highest state of perfection that a servant can achieve is when he is praising and thanking Allāh: the Messenger of Allāh (صَلَّىاللهُعَلَيْهِوَسَلَّمَ) said:

$$إِنَّ اللَّهَ لَيَرْضَى عَنِ الْعَبْدِ أَنْ يَأْكُلَ الأَكْلَةَ فَيَحْمَدَهُ عَلَيْهَا أَوْ يَشْرَبَ الشَّرْبَةَ فَيَحْمَدَهُ عَلَيْهَا$$

"Allāh will be pleased with His slave who praises Him (i.e., says *al-hamdu lillāh*) when he eats and praises Him when he drinks."[12]

And when the Messenger of Allāh (صَلَّىاللهُعَلَيْهِوَسَلَّمَ) would retire to bed, he would say:

---

[12] Reported by Muslim (2734)

الْحَمْدُ لِلَّهِ الَّذِي أَطْعَمَنَا وَسَقَانَا، وَكَفَانَا وَآوَانَا، كَمْ مَنْ لَا كَافَّ لَهُ وَلَا مُؤْوِيَ

"Praise is due to Allāh Who has fed us, provided us drink, satisfied us, and gave us protection. Many are those who have no one to provide for them or give them shelter)."[13]

And "Rabbul *'Ālamīn*" **(The Lord of all that exists)** (1:1)), contains Faith in the *Rubūbiyyah* of Allāh (Singling out Allāh in His actions). The Lord is The King, The Creator, The Sustainer, The Director, The Disposer of Affairs, The Giver of Life, The Taker of Life, The Withholder, The Granter, He is the Who humbles, lowers, raises, exalts, honors, and humiliates (any of His creation). He disposes of all the affairs in this universe. He (سُبْحَانَهُ وَتَعَالَى) brought it into existence from nothing, and He (عَزَّوَجَلَّ) is The One Who governs over all matters throughout the creation as He wills and imposes in it what He wishes; none can repel His order, and none can put back His judgment:

﴿ قُلِ ٱللَّهُمَّ مَٰلِكَ ٱلْمُلْكِ تُؤْتِى ٱلْمُلْكَ مَن تَشَآءُ وَتَنزِعُ ٱلْمُلْكَ مِمَّن تَشَآءُ وَتُعِزُّ مَن تَشَآءُ وَتُذِلُّ مَن تَشَآءُ ۖ بِيَدِكَ ٱلْخَيْرُ ۖ إِنَّكَ عَلَىٰ كُلِّ شَىْءٍ قَدِيرٌ ۝ ﴾

---

[13] Reported by Muslim (2715)

"Say (O Muḥammad ﷺ): "O Allāh! Possessor of the kingdom, You give the kingdom to whom You will, and You take the kingdom from whom You will, and You endue with honor whom You will, and You humiliate whom You will. In Your Hand is all good. Verily, You are All-capable to do all things." [Sūrah Āli ʿImrān (3):26]

And Allāh (عَزَّوَجَلَّ) said:

﴿ قُلْ هُوَ ٱلْقَادِرُ عَلَىٰٓ أَن يَبْعَثَ عَلَيْكُمْ عَذَابًا مِّن فَوْقِكُمْ أَوْ مِن تَحْتِ أَرْجُلِكُمْ أَوْ يَلْبِسَكُمْ شِيَعًا وَيُذِيقَ بَعْضَكُم بَأْسَ بَعْضٍ ٱنظُرْ كَيْفَ نُصَرِّفُ ٱلْآيَٰتِ لَعَلَّهُمْ يَفْقَهُونَ ۝ ﴾

"Say: "He has the power to send torment on you from above or from under your feet, or to cover you with confusion in party strife, and make you taste the violence of one another." See how variously We explain the Āyāt (proofs, evidence, lessons, signs, revelations, etc.), so that they may understand." [Sūrah al-Anʿām (6):65]

The scholars said concerning the explanation of Allāh's (سُبْحَانَهُوَتَعَالَى) statement "**so that they may understand:**" It means, so they may understand the purpose of their creation and what they were brought into existence to actualize, as it pertains to the exclusive worship of Allāh and having sincerity in the religion for Him (سُبْحَانَهُوَتَعَالَى).

"**...Torment on you from above,**" the scholars said: [torment] the likes of destructive storms and strong winds. "**...Or from under**

your feet," like earthquakes and sinkholes and what is similar to these from the different types of punishments—so Allāh is Capable of all things; it is His affair, it is His creation, and it is all under His disposal. Thus, if the Muslim understands this meaning, it is not possible for him to direct his worship and hope to other than The Lord, The One Who is Deservedly Praised (سُبْحَانَهُوَتَعَالَى).

This is why it is from ignorance and misguidance for some people to say concerning earthquakes that they are natural phenomena or attribute them to the earth itself or something similar because this is the Dominion of Allāh and He (سُبْحَانَهُوَتَعَالَى) deals with it as He wishes and Allāh (سُبْحَانَهُوَتَعَالَى) has said in the *Qur'ān*:

$$ \text{﴿ وَمَا نُرْسِلُ بِٱلْآيَٰتِ إِلَّا تَخْوِيفًا ۝ ﴾} $$

"And We sent not the signs except to warn, and to make them afraid (of destruction)." [Sūrah al-Isrā (17):59]

Meaning, Allāh uses His Enormous Signs to frighten His servants so that they may remember, so that they may understand, and so that they may repent to Allāh (سُبْحَانَهُوَتَعَالَى).

Therefore, the servant's Faith in this requires that he singles out his worship and sincerity in the religion for This Lord (سُبْحَانَهُوَتَعَالَى); and this is The Straight Path of Allāh, as Allāh (سُبْحَانَهُوَتَعَالَى) said:

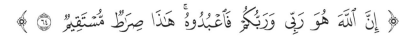

$$ \text{﴿ إِنَّ ٱللَّهَ هُوَ رَبِّي وَرَبُّكُمْ فَٱعْبُدُوهُ هَٰذَا صِرَٰطٌ مُّسْتَقِيمٌ ۝ ﴾} $$

"Verily, Allāh! He is my Lord (God) and your Lord. So, worship Him (Alone). This is the (only) Straight Path (i.e., Allāh's religion of true Islāmic Monotheism)." [Sūrah az-Zukhruf (43):64]

So, there is no partner for Allāh, not even in the weight of an atom from this universe.

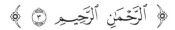

"The Most Gracious, the Most Merciful (1:2)):"

He (سُبْحَانَهُوَتَعَالَى) has the attribute of mercy towards His servants because all the Names of Allāh (عَزَّوَجَلَّ) are proof for the affirmation of perfect attributes for Him (جَلَّوَعَلَا).

On the authority of 'Umar Ibn al-Khattāb (رضي الله عنه) who said:

قَدِمَ عَلَى النَّبِيِّ صلى الله عليه وسلم سَبْيٌ، فَإِذَا امْرَأَةٌ مِنَ السَّبْيِ قَدْ تَحْلُبُ ثَدْيَهَا تَسْقِي، إِذَا وَجَدَتْ صَبِيًّا فِي السَّبْيِ أَخَذَتْهُ فَأَلْصَقَتْهُ بِبَطْنِهَا وَأَرْضَعَتْهُ، فَقَالَ لَنَا النَّبِيُّ صلى الله عليه وسلم "أَتَرَوْنَ هَذِهِ طَارِحَةً وَلَدَهَا فِي النَّارِ". قُلْنَا لاَ وَهْىَ تَقْدِرُ عَلَى أَنْ لاَ تَطْرَحَهُ. فَقَالَ "اللَّهُ أَرْحَمُ بِعِبَادِهِ مِنْ هَذِهِ بِوَلَدِهَا

"Some *Sabi* (i.e., war prisoners, children and woman only) were brought before the Prophet (صَلَّىٱللَّهُعَلَيْهِوَسَلَّمَ) and behold, a woman amongst them was milking her breasts to feed

and whenever she found a child amongst the captives, she took it over her chest and nursed it (she had lost her child but later she found him) the Prophet said to us: 'Do you think that this woman would throw her son in the fire?' We replied: 'No, not if she has the power not to throw him (in the fire).' The Prophet (ﷺ) then said: 'Allāh is more merciful to His slaves than this lady to her son."[14]

And His Mercy engulfs everything; He (عَزَّوَجَلَّ) has written it for the people of Faith and the people of repentance who hope for His Mercy and fear His Punishment. So, if you know that your Lord is the Most Merciful and that His Mercy reaches everything, then you realize how desperately your soul requires His Mercy. Thus, you should ask Allāh (عَزَّوَجَلَّ) to make you from those who are covered by His Mercy.

And His statement,

$$﴿ إِيَّاكَ نَعْبُدُ وَإِيَّاكَ نَسْتَعِينُ ﴾$$

"You (Alone) we worship, and You (Alone) we ask for help (for each and everything)" (1:4), means, O Allāh for You Alone we specify our worship. We single You Out Alone for seeking assistance. So, we do not worship except Allāh, and we only ask for help from Allāh—and this is the *Tawhīd* of Allāh in worship. **"You Alone We worship,"** the object (You) being mentioned first here

---

[14] Reported by al-Bukhārī (5999) and Muslim (2754)

serves the purpose of specifying only Allāh for deification, meaning, we worship You and no one else. And "**And You (Alone) we ask for help,**" meaning, we ask You only for help and one else. And if you come to realize this, then you know your dire need for and dependence upon Allāh and that you cannot afford to be without Him for a blink of an eye. If Allāh does not aid you, you will not be able to move or fulfill your needs and deeds, nor will you be able to perform acts of worship or obedience.

The Prophet (ﷺ) said to Mu'ādh Ibn Jabal (ﷺ):

"O Mu'ādh, By Allāh, I love you and advise you not to miss supplicating after every *Salāh* (prayer) saying:

اللّٰهُمَّ أَعِنِّي على ذِكْرِكَ وَشُكرِكَ، وَحُسْنَ عِبَادَتِكَ

"O Allāh, help me remember You, express gratitude to You and worship You in the best manner)."[15]

And he (ﷺ) said:

اِحْرِصْ عَلَى مَا يَنْفَعُكَ وَاسْتَعِنْ بِاللهِ

"Be diligent in what will benefit you and seek assistance from Allāh."[16]

---

[15] Reported by Abū Dāwūd (1522) and authenticated by al-Albānī (رحمه الله) in *Sahīh Sunan Abī Dāwūd* (1/417)

[16] A segment from the *Hadīth* reported by Muslim (2664)

"**You Alone We worship,**" is a fulfillment of the statement, "*Lā ilāha illallāh*" (There is no god worthy of worship except Allāh); and "**And You (Alone) we ask for help,**" is a fulfillment of the statement, "*Lā howla wa lā quwwata illā billāh*" (There is no might or power except with Allāh); because "*Lā ilāha illallāh*" embodies singling out Allāh Alone in worship and "*Lā howla wa lā quwwata illā billāh*" represents singling out Allāh Alone in seeking help from. Thus, it is apparent ignorance and a grave error that a person recites,

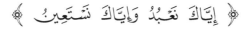

"**You (Alone) we worship, and You (Alone) we ask for help (for each and everything),**" then stretches out his hands saying: "Support me O so and so, relieve me O so and so," turning to someone from the creation like himself who has no power to give or prevent anything, nor possess sole-power of causing death, giving life and raising the dead for himself, let alone doing it for anyone else. Where does the one who calls upon other than Allāh—whether it is a prophet, a saint, a righteous person, or a wicked person—stand with regards to His statement: "**You (Alone) we worship?**" Where is he from it?! Because the meaning of "**You (Alone) we worship**" is: Only You O Allāh we worship.

Worship encompasses *Salāh*, fasting, Hajj, sacrificing, and *Du'ā* as the Prophet said: "*Du'ā* (supplicating) is worship."[17] So if *Du'ā* is

---

[17] Reported by Abū Dāwūd (1479) and authenticated by al-Albānī (رحمه الله) in *Sahīh Sunan Abī Dāwūd* (1/407)

worship, how can it be directed to other than Allāh, and how can other than Allāh be called upon? And Allāh said:

$$﴿ قُلِ ٱدۡعُوا۟ ٱلَّذِينَ زَعَمۡتُم مِّن دُونِهِۦ فَلَا يَمۡلِكُونَ كَشۡفَ ٱلضُّرِّ عَنكُمۡ وَلَا تَحۡوِيلًا ٥٦ ﴾$$

"Say (O Muḥammad ﷺ): "Call upon those - besides Him - whom you pretend [to be gods like angels, 'Isā (Jesus), 'Uzair (Ezra) and others]. They have neither the power to remove the adversity from you nor even to shift it from you to another person." [Sūrah al-Isrā (17): 56]

And Allāh (سُبۡحَانَهُۥوَتَعَالَى) said:

$$﴿ قُلِ ٱدۡعُوا۟ ٱلَّذِينَ زَعَمۡتُم مِّن دُونِ ٱللَّهِ لَا يَمۡلِكُونَ مِثۡقَالَ ذَرَّةٍ فِي ٱلسَّمَٰوَٰتِ وَلَا فِي ٱلۡأَرۡضِ وَمَا لَهُمۡ فِيهِمَا مِن شِرۡكٍ وَمَا لَهُۥ مِنۡهُم مِّن ظَهِيرٍ ٢٢ ﴾$$

"Say: (O Muḥammad ﷺ to those polytheists, pagans, etc.) "Call upon those whom you assert (to be associate gods) besides Allah, they possess not even the weight of an atom (or a small ant), either in the heavens or on the earth, nor have they any share in either, nor there is for Him any supporter from among them." [Sūrah Saba (34):22]

And Allāh (سُبْحَانَهُوَتَعَالَى) said:

﴿ إِن تَدْعُوهُمْ لَا يَسْمَعُواْ دُعَآءَكُمْ وَلَوْ سَمِعُواْ مَا ٱسْتَجَابُواْ لَكُمْ وَيَوْمَ ٱلْقِيَمَةِ يَكْفُرُونَ بِشِرْكِكُمْ وَلَا يُنَبِّئُكَ مِثْلُ خَبِيرٍ ﴿١٤﴾ ﴾

"If you invoke (or call upon) them, they hear not your call, and if (in case) they were to hear, they could not grant it (your request) to you. And on the Day of Resurrection, they will disown your worship of them. And none can inform you (O Muḥammad صَلَّىٱللَّهُعَلَيْهِوَسَلَّمَ) like Him Who is the All-Knower (of everything)." [Sūrah Fāṭir (35):14]

And Allāh (سُبْحَانَهُوَتَعَالَى) said:

﴿ وَمَنْ أَضَلُّ مِمَّن يَدْعُواْ مِن دُونِ ٱللَّهِ مَن لَّا يَسْتَجِيبُ لَهُۥ إِلَىٰ يَوْمِ ٱلْقِيَمَةِ وَهُمْ عَن دُعَآئِهِمْ غَفِلُونَ ﴿٥﴾ وَإِذَا حُشِرَ ٱلنَّاسُ كَانُواْ لَهُمْ أَعْدَآءً وَكَانُواْ بِعِبَادَتِهِمْ كَفِرِينَ ﴿٦﴾ ﴾

"And who is more astray than one who calls on besides Allāh, such as will not answer him till the Day of Resurrection, and who are (even) unaware of their calls (invocations) to them? And when mankind are gathered (on the Day of Resurrection), they (the false deities) will

**become their enemies and will deny their worshipping."
[Sūrah al-Ahqāf (46):5-6]**

Indeed, whoever understands "**You (Alone) we worship**" correctly, he will not turn to other than Allāh; it is not conceivable that he will seek help from other than Allāh. How can he possibly seek aid from a person who is unable to bring himself harm or benefit, nor grant himself something or take it away, and yet leave The One Who holds the reigns of everything in His hands and the keys to the heavens and earth—The One Whose Command, when He intends a thing, is only that he says to it, "Be!" and it is?! This *Sūrah* cultivates a person upon the *Tawhīd* of Allāh (عَزَّوَجَلَّ), only a person who understands its meanings and comprehends its content.

3RD GUIDELINE: SINCERITY & COMPLIANCE WITH THE SUNNAH

From the guidelines contained within this great *Sūrah* are the two conditions for the acceptance of acts of worship. Worship, no matter what it is, will not be accepted by Allāh (عَزَّوَجَلَّ) unless it fulfills two conditions; if they are both present, it will be accepted, but if both or one of them is absent, then the worship will be rejected. These two conditions are *al-Ikhlās* (sincerity of actions) for Allāh and *al-Mutāba'ah* (compliance) with the Messenger (صَلَّى ٱللَّهُ عَلَيْهِ وَسَلَّمَ).

Allāh will not accept the worship of a servant unless it is sincerely done for Him and according to the Sunnah of His Prophet (صَلَّى ٱللَّهُ عَلَيْهِ وَسَلَّمَ); so if *Ikhlās* and *Mutāba'ah* for the Messenger (عَلَيْهِ ٱلصَّلَاةُ وَٱلسَّلَامُ) are present in any act of worship, it will be accepted. If *Ikhlās* or *Mutāba'ah* is missing, it will be rejected. Allāh (سُبْحَانَهُ وَتَعَالَى) said in the Noble *Qur'ān*:

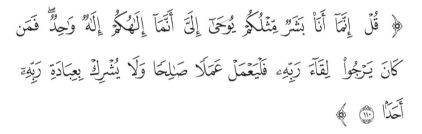

﴿ قُلْ إِنَّمَآ أَنَا۠ بَشَرٌ مِّثْلُكُمْ يُوحَىٰٓ إِلَيَّ أَنَّمَآ إِلَٰهُكُمْ إِلَٰهٌ وَٰحِدٌ فَمَن كَانَ يَرْجُوا۟ لِقَآءَ رَبِّهِۦ فَلْيَعْمَلْ عَمَلًا صَٰلِحًا وَلَا يُشْرِكْ بِعِبَادَةِ رَبِّهِۦٓ أَحَدًۢا ۝ ﴾

"Say (O Muḥammad ﷺ): "I am only a man like you. It has been revealed to me that your Ilāh (God) is One Ilāh (i.e., Allāh). So, whoever hopes for the Meeting with his Lord, let him work righteousness and associate none as a partner in the worship of his Lord." [Sūrah al-Kahf (18): 110]

Allāh (جَلَّ وَعَلَا) mentioned both conditions in this verse, He (سُبْحَانَهُ وَتَعَالَى) said, "**let him work righteousness.**" The deeds will not be righteousness unless they are in conformity with the Sunnah, the way of the Prophet (ﷺ) because he is the one who clarified to the nation what a righteous good deed is:

$$\text{﴿ وَإِنَّكَ لَتَهْدِى إِلَىٰ صِرَٰطٍ مُّسْتَقِيمٍ ۞ صِرَٰطِ ٱللَّهِ ٱلَّذِى لَهُۥ مَا فِى ٱلسَّمَٰوَٰتِ وَمَا فِى ٱلْأَرْضِ أَلَآ إِلَى ٱللَّهِ تَصِيرُ ٱلْأُمُورُ ۞ ﴾}$$

"And verily, you (O Muḥammad ﷺ) are indeed guiding (mankind) to the Straight Path (i.e., Allāh's Religion of Islāmic Monotheism). The Path of Allāh, to Whom belongs all that is in the heavens and all that is in the earth. Verily, all the matters at the end go to Allāh (for decision)." [Sūrah ash-Shūrā (42):53]

[Going back to the verse in Sūrah al-Kahf], Allāh (سُبْحَانَهُ وَتَعَالَى) mentioned the following condition in His statement: "**...And associate none as a partner in the worship of his Lord.**" This is concerning *Ikhlās,* and it is that the doer of the deed frees and disassociates himself from *Shirk* (polytheism, associating partners with Allāh) by having sincerity for Allāh. And *Shirk* is equating others with Allāh in matters that are exclusively for Allāh, whether it is in His worship, unique actions, or Names and Attributes. So, these are the two conditions for the acceptance of deeds.

Allāh (سُبْحَانَهُوَتَعَالَى) said:

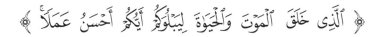

"Who has created death and life, that He may test you which of you is best in deeds." [Sūrah al-Mulk (67):2]

Notice here that Allāh did not say, "**...that He may test you which of you performs more deed**," since what is given consideration to is the quality. A deed will not be of good quality accept with the fulfillment of these two conditions. For this reason, al-Fuḍayl Ibn ʿIyāḍ (رَحِمَهُ أَللَّهُ) said concerning the statement of Allāh (سُبْحَانَهُوَتَعَالَى): "**...that He may test you which of you is best in deeds**," it means, "it is most sincere and sound." It was said to him: "O Abū ʿAlī, what 'it is most sincere sound?'" He replied: "If a deed is done sincerely but is not sound, it will not be accepted, and if it is sound but not sincere, it will not be accepted; until it is both sincere and sound. And the sincere deed is that which is done only for Allāh and the sound deed is that which is in compliance with the Sunnah."

These two excellent conditions for the acceptance of deeds are found in *Sūrah al-Fātihah*:

The condition of *Ikhlās* (Sincerity): It is located in His (سُبْحَانَهُوَتَعَالَى) statement: "**You Alone we worship.**" The one who the action is done for here (Allāh) is placed at the front, and this signifies exclusivity. Therefore, the meaning of "**You Alone we worship,**" is, "We exclusively make our acts of obedience for You, we will not direct anything of worship to other than You." So '*al-Khālis*' (derived from *Ikhlās*) means pure and unmixed and if you want to further understand what *Ikhlās* means in the Arabic language, then read the statement of Allāh in *Sūrah an-Nahl*:

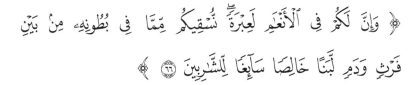

"**And verily! There is a lesson for you in the cattle. We give you to drink of that which is in their bellies, from between excretions and blood, pure (Khālis) milk, palatable to the drinkers.**" [Sūrah an-Nahl (16):66]

Meaning, it is untainted and clean; and milk comes from the udders of cattle through excretions and blood. It is said that during the milking process, the liquid comes out from between secretions and blood. However, it pours out pure without any drops of blood and feces—blessed be Allāh, the Best of Creators. And having *Ikhlās* in worship means that the deification is pure and untainted; only the Face of Allāh is intended with it.

It has been reported in a *Hadīth Qudsī* [18] that Allāh (عَزَّوَجَلَّ) said:

أَنَا أَغْنَى الشُّرَكَاءِ عَنِ الشِّرْكِ؛ مَنْ عَمِلَ عَمَلًا أَشْرَكَ مَعِي غَيْرِي، تَرَكْتُهُ وَشِرْكَهُ

"I am the One Who is most free from want of partners. He who does a thing for the sake of someone else besides Me, I discard him and his polytheism."[19]

And the Messenger of Allāh (صَلَّ ٱللَّهُ عَلَيْهِ وَسَلَّمَ) said:

أَلَا أُخْبِرُكُمْ بِمَا هُوَ أَخْوَفُ عَلَيْكُمْ عِنْدِي مِنَ الْمَسِيحِ الدَّجَّالِ ". قَالَ قُلْنَا بَلَى . فَقَالَ " الشِّرْكُ الْخَفِيُّ أَنْ يَقُومَ الرَّجُلُ يُصَلِّي فَيُزَيِّنُ صَلَاتَهُ لِمَا يَرَى مِنْ نَظَرِ رَجُلٍ

"Shall I not tell you of that which I fear more for you than the *Dajjāl* (Anti-Christ)? Hidden polytheism: When a man stands to pray and makes it look good because he sees a man looking at him."[20]

---

[18] It is a *Hadīth* in which the Messenger is relating the direct speech of Allāh (جَلَّ وَعَلَا)
[19] Reported by Muslim (2985)
[20] Reported by Ibn Mājah (4204) and graded *Hasan* by al-Albānī (رَحِمَهُٱللَّهُ) in *Sahīh Sunan Ibn Mājah* (3408)

And the Messenger (صَلَّى اللَّهُ عَلَيْهِ وَسَلَّمَ) said: "O people fear this *Shirk* (Polytheism), for certain, it is more hidden than the creeping of ants. Say:

اللَّهُمَّ إِنَّا نَعُوذُ بِكَ مِن أَنْ نُشْرِكَ بِكَ شَيْئًا نَعْلَمُهُ، وَنَسْتَغْفِرُكَ لِمَا لاَ نَعْلَمُ

'O Allāh, we seek refuge with You from knowingly associating anything with You [in worship], and we seek Your forgiveness from doing it unknowingly.'"[21]

Thus, it is incumbent upon the servant to be entirely cautious from *Shirk* and seek refuge with Allāh (تَبَارَكَ وَتَعَالَى) from falling into *Shirk*. He must observe this tremendous Prophetic supplication that the Prophet (صَلَّى اللَّهُ عَلَيْهِ وَسَلَّمَ) has taught his nation.

The second condition (*al-Mutāba'ah*): It has come in His Allāh's (سُبْحَانَهُ وَتَعَالَى) statement:

﴿ اهْدِنَا الصِّرَاطَ الْمُسْتَقِيمَ ۝ صِرَاطَ الَّذِينَ أَنْعَمْتَ عَلَيْهِمْ غَيْرِ الْمَغْضُوبِ عَلَيْهِمْ وَلَا الضَّالِّينَ ۝ ﴾

"Guide us to the Straight Way. The Way of those on whom You have bestowed Your Grace, not (the way) of those who earned Your Anger (such as the Jews), nor of those

---

[21] Reported by Ahmad (4/403) and graded *Hasan Li Ghayrihi* by al-Albānī (رَحِمَهُ اللَّهُ) in *Sahīh at-Targhīb* (36)

who went astray (such as the Christians).” [Sūrah al-Fātihah (1):5-7]

This contains proof that Allāh does not accept a deed unless it is by the light of the Straight Way, which the Prophet (ﷺ) has called to. It has authentically been reported in a *Hadīth* that the Prophet (ﷺ) said:

مَنْ عَمِلَ عَمَلًا لَيْسَ عَلَيْهِ أَمْرُنَا فَهُوَ رَدٌّ

“Whoever performs a deed that is not in compliance with our affair (i.e., Islām), will have it rejected.”[22]

Meaning that it will be discarded and returned back to its doer unaccepted. For this reason, he has also said: “Pray as you have seen me pray.”[23]

And he said in Hajj:

لِتَأْخُذُوا عَنِّي مَنَاسِكَكُمْ

“Learn your rituals (by seeing me performing them).”[24]

There is no room for you to strive and say, “This is more virtuous” or “this is better;” instead, the Sunnah and the guidance of your

---

[22] Reported by Muslim
[23] Reported by al-Bukhārī (631)
[24] Reported by Muslim (1297)

noble Prophet (ﷺ) is sufficient for you. And the Prophet (ﷺ) when giving a sermon on Friday would say:

أَمَّا بَعْدُ، فَإِنَّ خَيْرَ الْـحَدِيثِ كِتَابُ اللهِ، وَخَيْرَ الْهَدِي هَدِي مُحَمَّدٍ صَلَّى اللهُ عَلَيْهِ وَسَلَّمَ.

"As to what follows, verily, the best of speech is the Book of Allāh, and the best of guidance is the guidance of Muḥammad (ﷺ)." [25]

Therefore, there is no guidance more complete than his guidance; there is no methodology better than his; there is no approach better than his (ﷺ). And this *Sūrah* contains the application of these two conditions.

---

[25] Reported by Muslim (867)

4TH GUIDELINE: THE STRAIGHT PATH

The discussion concerning the Straight Path—which is from the guidelines of this blessed *Sūrah*—will be limited to the following points:

- ❖ Guidance to the Straight Path is a favor from Allāh.
- ❖ What is the Straight Path?
- ❖ Obstacles on the Straight Path
- ❖ Who are the people of this Straight Path?

1. Guidance to the Straight Path is a favor from Allāh.

Allāh is the One Who Guides; He guides whomever He wills and leads whomever He wills astray. Allāh (عَزَّوَجَلَّ) said:

﴿ وَٱللَّهُ يَدۡعُوٓاْ إِلَىٰ دَارِ ٱلسَّلَٰمِ وَيَهۡدِى مَن يَشَآءُ إِلَىٰ صِرَٰطٍ مُّسۡتَقِيمٍ ۝ ﴾

"Allāh calls to the Home of peace (i.e., Paradise, by accepting Allāh's religion of Islāmic Monotheism and by doing righteous good deeds and abstaining from polytheism and evil deeds) and guides whom He wills to a Straight Path." [Sūrah Yūnus (10):25]

In another verse, Allāh (سُبْحَانَهُوَتَعَالَى) says:

﴿ أَفَمَن زُيِّنَ لَهُ سُوٓءُ عَمَلِهِۦ فَرَءَاهُ حَسَنًا فَإِنَّ ٱللَّهَ يُضِلُّ مَن يَشَآءُ وَيَهْدِى مَن يَشَآءُ ﴾

"Is he, then, to whom the evil of his deeds made fair-seeming, so that he considers it as good (equal to one who is rightly guided)? Verily, Allāh sends astray whom He wills and guides whom He wills." [Sūrah Fātir (35):8]

So, guidance is in the Hands of Allāh (سُبْحَانَهُوَتَعَالَى). How dire is our need…how urgent is our need…how pressing is our need in always beseeching The Lord (سُبْحَانَهُوَتَعَالَى) to guide us to the Straight Path. And in the *Du'ā al-Qunūt*[26] [are the words]:

اللَّهُمَّ اهْدِنِي فِيمَنْ هَدَيْتَ

"O Allāh, guide me with those You have guided."[27]

And in the *Hadīth* of 'Alī who said: "The Messenger of Allāh (صَلَّىٰاللَّهُعَلَيْهِوَسَلَّمَ) said to me: 'Say:

---

[26] **Translator's note**: It is a supplication made in the Witr (odd) prayer offered at night.
[27] Reported by Abū Dāwūd (1425) and authenticated by al-Albānī (رَحِمَهُٱللَّهُ) in *Sahīh Sunan Abī Dāwūd* (1/392)

اللَّهُمَّ اهْدِنِي وَسَدِّدْنِي

'O Allāh, I ask you for guidance and steadfastness upon guidance.'"28

And in the *Hadīth* of al-Barā, the Messenger of Allāh (صَلَّى اللهُ عَلَيْهِ وَسَلَّمَ) said on the day of *al-Khandaq* (the Battle of the Trench):

اللَّهُمَّ لَوْلاَ أَنتَ مَا اهْتَدَيْنَا وَلاَ تَصَدَّقْنَا وَلاَ صَلَّيْنَا

"O Allāh, without You, we would not have been guided, neither would we have given in charity, nor would we have prayed."29

Therefore, guidance is in the Hands of Allāh, and He (سُبْحَانَهُ وَتَعَالَى) guides whomever He wills to His Straight Path. If your Lord does not grant you guidance to His Straight Path, you will go astray in this world; because this world is full of trials, tribulations, and distractions like the devil, evil companions, and the inclined self to evil. Thus, it was said:

"The amazement is not in how the ruined person came to perish, rather in how the saved one came to be saved;"

This is because the repelling and destructive factors are many, and none can be guarded against Allāh's affair except whomever He has

---

28 Reported by Muslim (2725)
29 Reported by al-Bukhārī (3034) and Muslim (1803)

mercy on; guidance is from His Grace (سُبْحَانَهُوَتَعَالَى). So, you know yourself and that you are desperately in need of Allāh guiding you to His Straight Path.

2. What is the straight Path?

The Straight Path is the path that has no crookedness or curves or slants to the right or left; the Messenger of Allāh (صَلَّىٱللَّهُعَلَيْهِوَسَلَّمَ) said:

قَدْ تَرَكْتُكُمْ عَلَى الْبَيْضَاءِ لَيْلُهَا كَنَهَارِهَا لاَ يَزِيغُ عَنْهَا بَعْدِي إِلاَّ هَالِكٌ

"I am leaving you upon a (path of) brightness whose night is like its day. No one will deviate from it after I am gone, but one who is doomed."[30]

And Ibn Mas'ūd (رَضِيَاللَّهُعَنْهُ) was asked:

مَا هُوَ الصِّرَاطُ الْمُسْتَقِيمُ؟ قَالَ: هُوَ طَرِيٌّ تَرَكَنَا النَّبِيُّ صَلَّى اللهُ عَلَيْهِ وَسَلَّمَ فِي أَوَّلِهِ، وَآخِرِهِ فِ] الْـجَنَّةِ، وَعَلَى جَنْبَتَيْ الطَّرِيقِ عَنْ يَمِينِهِ، عَنْ شِمَالِهِ جَوَاد.

"What is the Straight Path?" He said: "It is a path upon which the Prophet (صَلَّىٱللَّهُعَلَيْهِوَسَلَّمَ) has left us in its beginning,

---

[30] Reported by Ibn Mājah (43) and authenticated by al-Albānī (رَحِمَهُٱللَّهُ) in *Sahīh Sunan Ibn Mājah* (41)

and its end is in Paradise, and on the two sides of the path—its right and left—are [other] paths."

The Prophet (ﷺ) has clarified this path with a parable that he gave to the companions.

فَخَطَّ خَطًّا وَخَطَّ خَطَّيْنِ عَنْ يَمِينِهِ وَخَطَّ خَطَّيْنِ عَنْ يَسَارِهِ ثُمَّ وَضَعَ يَدَهُ فِي الْخَطِّ الْأَوْسَطِ فَقَالَ " هَذَا سَبِيلُ اللَّهِ " .

He drew one line and two lines on its right and two other lines on its left. He then placed his hand on the black line and said: "This is the Path of Allāh," and read this verse:

﴿ وَأَنَّ هَٰذَا صِرَٰطِى مُسْتَقِيمًا فَٱتَّبِعُوهُ وَلَا تَتَّبِعُوا۟ ٱلسُّبُلَ فَتَفَرَّقَ بِكُمْ عَن سَبِيلِهِۦ ﴾

"And verily, this is my Straight Path, so follow it, and follow not (other) paths, for they will separate you away from His Path." [Sūrah al-An'ām (6):153] [31]

Because the devil is sitting in wait for the servant in his Straight Path wanting him to turn to the right or left:

---

[31] Reported by Ibn Mājah (11) and authenticated by al-Albānī (رحمه الله) in *Sahīh Sunan Ibn Mājah* (11)

قَالَ فَمَا أَغْوَيْتَنِى لَأَقْعُدَنَّ لَهُمْ صِرَاطَكَ ٱلْمُسْتَقِيمَ ۝ ثُمَّ لَآتِيَنَّهُم مِّنْ بَيْنِ أَيْدِيهِمْ وَمِنْ خَلْفِهِمْ وَعَنْ أَيْمَٰنِهِمْ وَعَن شَمَآئِلِهِمْ ۝ وَلَا تَجِدُ أَكْثَرَهُمْ شَٰكِرِينَ ۝

"(Iblīs (Satan)) said: "Because You have sent me astray, surely, I will sit in wait against them (human beings) on Your Straight Path. Then I will come to them from before them and behind them, from their right and from their left, and You will not find most of them as thankful ones (i.e., they will not be dutiful to You)." [Sūrah al-'Arāf (7):16-17]

This is why it is reported in the *Hadīth* of Sabrah Ibn Abī Fākih:

إِنَّ الشَّيْطَانَ قَعَدَ لِابْنِ آدَمَ بِأَطْرُقِهِ

"Indeed, Satan sits in the paths of the son of Adam,"[32]

Meaning every path, the son of Adam takes, Satan will be sitting there; because he wants to deviate him and turn him away from the truth and guidance:

---

[32] Reported by an-Nasā'ī (3134) and authenticated by al-Albānī (رَحِمَهُ اللَّه) in *Sahīh Sunan an-Nasā'ī* (2/381)

﴿ ثُمَّ لَآتِيَنَّهُم مِّنۢ بَيْنِ أَيْدِيهِمْ وَمِنْ خَلْفِهِمْ وَعَنْ أَيْمَٰنِهِمْ وَعَن شَمَآئِلِهِمْ ۖ وَلَا تَجِدُ أَكْثَرَهُمْ شَٰكِرِينَ ﴿١٧﴾ ﴾

"Then I will come to them from before them and behind them, from their right and from their left, and You will not find most of them as thankful ones (i.e., they will not be dutiful to You)." [Sūrah al-'Arāf (7):17]

And most of the creation has died upon disbelief and ungratefulness to Allāh (سُبْحَانَهُ وَتَعَالَى):

﴿ وَمَآ أَكْثَرُ ٱلنَّاسِ وَلَوْ حَرَصْتَ بِمُؤْمِنِينَ ﴿١٠٣﴾ ﴾

"And most of mankind will not believe even if you desire it eagerly." [Sūrah Yūsuf (12):103]

There is another fantastic parable that the Prophet (صَلَّى اللَّهُ عَلَيْهِ وَسَلَّمَ) has made to clarify Allāh's Straight Path: On the authority of an-Nawwās Ibn Sam'ān al-Ansārī who reported that the Messenger of Allāh (صَلَّى اللَّهُ عَلَيْهِ وَسَلَّمَ) said:

ضَرَبَ اللهُ - تَعَالَى - مَثَلاً صِرَاطًا مُستَقِيمًا، وَعَلَى جَنبَتَيِ الصِّرَاطِ سُورَانِ فِيهِمَا أَبوَابٌ مُفَتَّحَةٌ، وَعَلَى الأَبوَابِ سُتُورٌ مُرخَاةٌ، وَعَلَى بَابِ الصِّرَاطِ دَاعٍ يَقُولُ: يَا أَيُّهَا النَّاسُ، ادخُلُوا الصِّرَاطَ جَمِيعًا وَلَا تَتَعَوَّجُوا، وَدَاعٍ يَدعُو مِن فَوقِ الصِّرَاطِ، فَإِذَا أَرَادَ الإِنسَانُ أَن يَفتَحَ شَيئًا مِن تِلكَ الأَبوَابِ

قَالَ: وَيْحَكَ لَا تَفْتَحْهُ، فَإِنَّكَ إِنْ تَفْتَحْهُ تَلِجْهُ، فَالصِّرَاطُ الإِسْلَامُ،

وَالسُّورَانِ حُدُودُ اللهِ ـ تَعَالَى ـ وَالأَبْوَابُ الْمُفَتَّحَةُ مَحَارِمُ اللهِ ـ تَعَالَى ـ

وَذَلِكَ الدَّاعِي عَلَى رَأْسِ الصِّرَاطِ كِتَابُ اللهِ ـ عَزَّ وَجَلَّ ـ وَالدَّاعِي مِن

فَوْقُ وَاعِظُ اللهِ فِي قَلْبِ كُلِّ مُسْلِمٍ

"Allāh has made a parable of the Straight Path: At the sides of the path, there are two walls with open doors, and the doors have open curtains. There is a caller at the head of the path calling: 'O people, all of you, enter the Straight Path and do not zigzag;' and a caller above the Straight Path calling. If one wants to open any of the doors, he says: 'Woe to you, do not open it! Verily, if you open it, you will enter it.' The Path is Islām; the two walls which are on the sides of the path are the legal limitations of Allāh, and the open doors are the things made inviolable by Allāh; the one calling at the head of the Path is the Book of Allāh; the one calling from above the Path is the preacher of Allāh in the heart of every Muslim."[33]

This is a preacher that Allāh has created to caution the Muslim in his heart to prevent him from falling into unlawful acts. Although, this admonisher might become corrupt if a person becomes immersed in the illegal actions; it will get to a state where it does

---

[33] Reported by Ahmad (4/182-183) and authenticated by al-Albānī (رَحِمَهُ ٱللَّه) in *Dhilāl al-Jannah Fī Takhrīj as-Sunnah* by Ibn Abī 'Āsim (19)

not recognize the good nor reject the evil, as the Lord (جَلَّ وَعَلَا) has said:

﴿ كَلَّا بَلْ رَانَ عَلَىٰ قُلُوبِهِم مَّا كَانُوا۟ يَكْسِبُونَ ۝ ﴾

Nay! But on their hearts is the *Rān* (covering of sins and evil deeds) which they used to earn. (al-Mutaffifīn: 14)

Meaning, it seals their hearts: "**...which they used to earn,**" from the sins and disobedience.

On the authority of Abū Hurairah (رضي الله عنه) who reported that the Messenger of Allāh (صَلَّى اللهُ عَلَيْهِ وَسَلَّمَ) said:

إِنَّ الْعَبْدَ إِذَا أَخْطَأَ خَطِيئَةً نُكِتَتْ فِي قَلْبِهِ نُكْتَةٌ سَوْدَاءُ فَإِذَا هُوَ نَزَعَ وَاسْتَغْفَرَ وَتَابَ سُقِلَ قَلْبُهُ وَإِنْ عَادَ زِيدَ فِيهَا حَتَّى تَعْلُوَ قَلْبَهُ وَهُوَ الرَّانُ الَّذِي ذَكَرَ اللهُ : ﴿ كَلَّا بَلْ رَانَ عَلَىٰ قُلُوبِهِم مَّا كَانُوا۟ يَكْسِبُونَ ۝ ﴾

"Verily, when the slave (of Allāh) commits a sin, a black spot appears on his heart. When he refrains from it, seeks forgiveness and repents, his heart is polished clean. But if he returns, it increases until it covers his entire heart. And that is the '*Rān*' which Allāh mentioned:

'Nay, but on their hearts is the *Rān* which they used to earn.' [Sūrah al-Mutaffifīn (83):14]'"

The point is that this is a wonderful parable for clarifying the Straight Path which was made as a similitude to Islām; it is a straight path with two walls on its sides, they are the legal limitations of Allāh—His Legislations that He has ordered His servants to remain steadfast upon and not transgress, as He (سُبْحَانَهُوَتَعَالَىٰ) has said:

$$﴿ تِلْكَ حُدُودُ ٱللَّهِ فَلَا تَعْتَدُوهَا ﴾$$

"These are the limits ordained by Allāh, so do not transgress them." [Sūrah al-Baqarah (2):229]

And the doors with the open curtains lead the one who enters through them to the impermissible limits; Allāh said in the other verse:

$$﴿ تِلْكَ حُدُودُ ٱللَّهِ فَلَا تَقْرَبُوهَا ﴾$$

"These are the limits set by Allāh, so approach them not." [Sūrah al-Baqarah (2):187]

What is meant by limits here is the prohibited matters, and what is meant by limits in the first verse is concerning what Allāh has allowed and legislated for His servants but ordered that they do not transgress and exceed them.

He (the Messenger) said: "**The doors have curtains,**" meaning the doors that lead one to commit something impressible. They have curtains that are raised and are without locks and keys, so minimal effort is needed to pass through them. And this is proof that falling into prohibited matters does not require much time or effort.

Just as there is a Straight Path that the servants are required to walk on, indeed, in front of them on the Day of Judgment is a Straight Path (a bridge); it will be erected over the *Matn* (brink, middle) of Hell and all the creation will be asked to cross it. Allāh (سُبْحَانَهُوَتَعَالَى) said:

﴿ وَإِن مِّنكُمْ إِلَّا وَارِدُهَا كَانَ عَلَىٰ رَبِّكَ حَتْمًا مَّقْضِيًّا ۞ ثُمَّ نُنَجِّى ٱلَّذِينَ ٱتَّقَوا وَّنَذَرُ ٱلظَّـٰلِمِينَ فِيهَا جِثِيًّا ۞ ﴾

"There is not one of you but will pass over it (Hell); this is with your Lord; a Decree which must be accomplished Then We shall save those who use to fear Allāh and were dutiful to Him. And We shall leave the Zālimūn (polytheists and wrongdoers) therein (humbled) to their knees (in Hell)." [Sūrah Maryam (19):71-72]

The path to Paradise is over this bridge, a bridge that is thinner than a strand of hair erected over the brink of Hell; and its fire will be blazing fiercely under the people, and they will be required to cross this bridge; Allāh has sworn by this:

﴿ وَإِن مِّنكُمْ إِلَّا وَارِدُهَا ﴾

"There is not one of you but will pass over it (Hell)." [Sūrah Maryam (19):71]

It is a must that this Straight Bridge over the middle of Hell is crossed. The Muslim is sure about this, however, he is doubtful about crossing it safely (and not falling into Hell); Allāh (جَلَّوَعَلَا) said:

$$\text{﴿ فَمَن زُحْزِحَ عَنِ ٱلنَّارِ وَأُدْخِلَ ٱلْجَنَّةَ فَقَدْ فَازَ وَمَا ٱلْحَيَوٰةُ ٱلدُّنْيَآ إِلَّا مَتَٰعُ ٱلْغُرُورِ ﴾ ﴿١٨٥﴾}$$

"And whoever is removed away from the Fire and admitted to Paradise, he indeed is successful. The life of this world is only the enjoyment of deception (a deceiving thing)." [Sūrah Āli ʿImrān (3):185]

So, he does not know, will he be from the successful ones who will be removed away from the Fire or not? Thus, it is befitting that the servant persists in remaining upon the Straight Path which is the Religion of Allāh—Islām—and not deviating from it to the right or left; Allāh (سُبْحَانَهُوَتَعَالَى) said:

$$\text{﴿ إِنَّ ٱلَّذِينَ قَالُوا۟ رَبُّنَا ٱللَّهُ ثُمَّ ٱسْتَقَٰمُوا۟ فَلَا خَوْفٌ عَلَيْهِمْ وَلَا هُمْ يَحْزَنُونَ ﴿١٣﴾ ﴾}$$

"Verily, those who say: "Our Lord is (only) Allāh," and after that stand firm (on the Islāmic Faith of Monotheism) on them shall be no fear, nor shall they grieve." [Sūrah al-Ahqāf (46):13]

'Umar Ibn al-Khattāb (ﷺ) said concerning "**and after that stand firm:**" "They do not skew and swerve like the swerving of the fox,"[34] meaning that they are firm upon treading the Straight Path of Allāh in this life, so their Lord will keep them firm on the Straight Path (bridge) that will be erected over the brink of Hell on the Day of Judgment.

3. Obstacles in treading the Straight Path:

It is incumbent for you to know—O voyager of this Path—that in front of you are obstacles that will prevent you from traveling on this Path and continuing upon it; and in short, they are three obstacles; and wonderful guidelines and blessed directives have come in this very *Sūrah* (*al-Fātihah*) on how to safely avoid them. They are obstacles that the people of knowledge have numerously drawn attention to and warned the people against them; their level of danger is following this order:

The 1st Obstacle: *Shirk* (associating partners with Allāh (سُبْحَانَهُوَتَعَالَى))

The 2nd Obstacle: Innovations [in the religion]

The 3rd Obstacle: Disobedience (sinning)

On the authority of 'Abdullāh Ibn Mas'ūd (ﷺ) who said that the Messenger of Allāh (صَلَّىٰاللَّهُعَلَيْهِوَسَلَّمَ) drew a line for us and said:

---

[34] Look in: *Tafsīr at-Tabarī (Sūrah Fussilat, 30)*

خَطَّ لَنَا رَسُولُ اللهِ صَلَّى اللهُ عَلَيْهِ وَسَلَّمَ خَطًّا، ثُمَّ قَالَ: هَذَا سَبِيلُ اللهِ،

ثُمَّ خَطَّ خُطُوطاً عَنْ يَمِينِهِ وَعَنْ شِمَالِهِ، ثُمَّ قَالَ: هَذِهِ سُبُلٌ مُتَفَرِّقَةٌ، عَلَى

كُلِّ سَبِيلٍ مِنْهَا شَيْطَانٌ يَدْعُو إِلَيْهِ، ثُمَّ قَرَأَ: ﴿ وَأَنَّ هَـٰذَا صِرَٰطِى

مُسْتَقِيمًا فَٱتَّبِعُوهُ وَلَا تَتَّبِعُوا۟ ٱلسُّبُلَ فَتَفَرَّقَ بِكُمْ عَن

سَبِيلِهِۦ ﴾

"This is the Path of Allāh," he then drew lines to its right and left and said: "These are different paths and upon everyone one of them is a devil calling to it." After that, he read:

"And verily, this (i.e., Allāh's Commandments mentioned in the above two Verses 151 and 152) is my Straight Path, so follow it, and follow not (other) paths, for they will separate you away from His Path." [Sūrah al-An'ām (7): 153][35]

And the different ways that the Prophet (ﷺ) mentioned are one of three: a path that will lead a person to commit *Shirk* with Allāh, or a path that will lead him to innovation or a way that will lead him to disobedience and sinning. And there is no doubt that the most beloved and desired of paths to Satan is that a person falls into

---

[35] Reported by Ahmad (1/435) and authenticated by al-Albānī (رَحِمَهُ اللَّهُ) in *at-Ta'līq 'Alā Hidāyah ar-Ruwāh* (1/131)

committing *Shirk* with Allāh; if he is not able to (get him to fall into this), then an innovation, if he is incapable, then into sinning; [if unsuccessful] he will move to what is less than these.

Hence, Ibn al-Qayyim mentioned in some of his books that what Satan desires from a human is seven matters and he will he give precedence to what is first, then the next; if he is unsuccessful in getting him to commit the greater one then he will move on to the lesser one. So the first sin that he wants a person to fall into is committing *Shirk* with Allāh (جَلَّ وَعَلَا); if he is unsuccessful, then he will want him to carry out an innovation because innovation is more beloved to the devil then sinning—why? Because the doer of innovation sees himself to be upon good while practicing his innovation and if it is said to him, "What you are upon is wrong, and it will not be accepted;" he will believe himself to be correct and upon the truth; whereas the sinner, if he is advised against his sin, he will know that he is wrong and committing a crime; thus he will say, "Supplicate to Allāh to accept my repentance, perhaps Allāh will forgive me." However, the innovator will not accept and be pleased [with the advice], instead, he will stand up for and defend his stance and persist in it; unless Allāh writes guidance for him and opens his heart to goodness.

For this reason, the Prophet (صَلَّى ٱللَّهُ عَلَيْهِ وَسَلَّمَ) has said:

إِنَّ اللهَ حَجَبَ التَّوْبَةَ عَنْ صَاحِبِ كُلِّ بِدْعَةٍ

"Allāh has blinded the doer of any innovation from repenting."[36]

Sins are divided into minor and major sins, and Allāh (سُبْحَانَهُوَتَعَالَى) says:

$$ \text{﴿ وَكُلُّ صَغِيرٍ وَكَبِيرٍ مُّسْتَطَرٌ ۞ ﴾} $$

"And everything, small and big, is written down (in al-Lawh al-Mahfūdh already beforehand, i.e., before it befalls, or is done by its doer: بالقدر الإيمان) (See the *Qur'ān* V.57:22 and its footnote)." [Sūrah al-Qamar (54):53]

Meaning: they are written against the servant, and he will find it in his record of deeds on the day when he will stand before Allāh (تَبَارَكَوَتَعَالَى):

$$ \text{﴿ وَيَقُولُونَ يَٰوَيْلَتَنَا مَالِ هَٰذَا ٱلْكِتَٰبِ لَا يُغَادِرُ صَغِيرَةً وَلَا} $$
$$ \text{كَبِيرَةً إِلَّآ أَحْصَٰهَا وَوَجَدُوا مَا عَمِلُوا حَاضِرًا وَلَا يَظْلِمُ رَبُّكَ} $$
$$ \text{أَحَدًا ۞ ﴾} $$

"They will say: "Woe to us! What sort of Book is this that leaves neither a small thing nor a big thing, but has recorded it with numbers?" And they will find all that they

---

[36] Reported by at-Tabarānī in *al-Awsad* (4202) and authenticated by al-Albānī (رَحِمَهُاللَّهُ) in *as-Sahīhah* (1620)

did, placed before them, and your Lord treats no one with injustice." [Sūrah al-Kahf (18):49]

If the devil is unable to get the servant to commit a major sin, he will strive in causing him to fall into a minor one; if he is unsuccessful in getting him to do this, he will strive in busying the servant from the acts of obedience and worship with the permissible matters; if he is unsuccessful at doing this, he will move on to the sixth level: busying him with matters that are less virtuous from the more meritorious ones—because the Religion of Allāh (عَزَّوَجَلَّ) and the acts of obedience which Allāh has commanded with are different in their levels of virtue; as the Prophet (صَلَّى ٱللَّهُ عَلَيْهِ وَسَلَّمَ) said:

الإِيمَانُ بِضْعٌ وَسَبْعُونَ شُعْبَةً فَأَفْضَلُهَا قَوْلُ لاَ إِلَهَ إِلاَّ اللَّهُ وَأَدْنَاهَا إِمَاطَةُ الأَذَى عَنِ الطَّرِيقِ

"Īmān (Faith) has over seventy branches, the most virtuous of which is the declaration: 'None has the right to be worshipped but Allāh'; and the least of which is the removal of harmful objects from the road."[37]

If he is unsuccessful with this sixth attempt, he will move on to a seventh matter—and no one is safe from this. If anyone was able to avoid this, it would have been the Messenger of Allāh (صَلَّى ٱللَّهُ عَلَيْهِ وَسَلَّمَ): It is that he will empower a soldier from his army to harm the person. If he despairs in deterring a person from goodness, he will send a

---

[37] Reported by al-Bukhārī (9) and Muslim (35) and this is his wording.

soldier from his army to mar him. Thus, this person will be exposed to some harm as a result of his nearness to Allāh (عَزَّوَجَلَّ). As a result, Allāh has ordered the believers to encourage each other with patience:

$$ ﴿ إِلَّا ٱلَّذِينَ ءَامَنُواْ وَعَمِلُواْ ٱلصَّٰلِحَٰتِ وَتَوَاصَوْاْ بِٱلْحَقِّ وَتَوَاصَوْاْ بِٱلصَّبْرِ ۝ ﴾ $$

"Except those who believe (in Islāmic Monotheism) and do righteous good deeds, and recommend one another to the truth (i.e., order one another to perform all kinds of good deeds (al-Ma'ruf) which Allāh has ordained, and abstain from all sorts of sins and evil acts (al-Munkar) which Allāh has forbidden), and recommend one another to patience (for the sufferings, harms, and injuries which one may encounter in Allāh's Cause while preaching His religion of Islāmic Monotheism or Jihād)." [Sūrah al-'Asr (103):3]

And He said:

$$ ﴿ وَتَوَاصَوْاْ بِٱلصَّبْرِ وَتَوَاصَوْاْ بِٱلْمَرْحَمَةِ ۝ ﴾ $$

"…and recommended one another to perseverance and patience, and (also) recommended one another to pity and compassion." [Sūrah al-Balad (90):17]

And this is because the harm that will afflict [a believer]—especially the one strong in Faith—is severe.

These are the steps that Satan gradually takes to get to a servant; and concerning this matter, read the statement of Allāh (سُبْحَانَهُوَتَعَالَ):

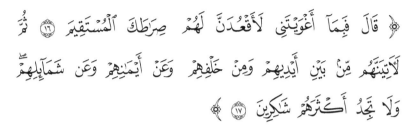

"(Iblīs) said: "Because You have sent me astray, surely I will sit in wait against them (human beings) on Your Straight Path (16) Then I will come to them from before them and behind them, from their right and from their left, and You will not find most of them as thankful ones (i.e., they will not be dutiful to You)." [Sūrah al-A'rāf (7):16-17]

And Satan is an enemy that sees you, but you do not see him—he is heavily equipped:

﴿ إِنَّهُۥ يَرَىٰكُمْ هُوَ وَقَبِيلُهُۥ مِنْ حَيْثُ لَا تَرَوْنَهُمْ ﴾

"Verily, he and Qabīluhu (his soldiers from the jinn or his tribe) see you from where you cannot see them." [Sūrah al-A'rāf (7):27]

He is sitting in wait for you on the Straight Path of Allāh to deter, avert and distance you from it, and to make you fall into the deep bottomless pits of misguidance—O Allāh we seek protection us from the accursed Satan.

So these three obstacles: *Shirk*, innovation, and sin; it is a must that every Muslim, male or female, be strictly cautious of them and fear for himself from falling into them; and they must seek guidance concerning this from the directives of *Sūrah al-Fātihah*, the *Qur'ān* and the *Sunnah* of the noble Prophet (ﷺ).

It was said to Abū Hurairah (رضى الله عنه):

> **"Inform us about what is *Taqwā*?"** He responded to the questioner: **"Have you taken a trail that has thorns?"** He said: **"Yes."** He asked: **"What will you do?"** He said: **"If I see a thorn, I will avoid it by going to its right or left, and I will be cautious about walking over it."** He (Abū Hurairah) said: **"This is *Taqwā* of Allāh (fear, God-consciousness).**

However, what you are cautious of here (*Taqwā*) is not thorns. It is more destructive than this to the human being: It is *Shirk*, innovation, and sin. So, the one traveling on the Straight Path of Allāh needs to be conscious and fearful and cautious of these matters. Some of the *Salaf* (righteous predecessors) said: "How can a person fear and avoid something that he has no knowledge of?" So it is required of you to know what *Shirk* is, to understand what innovation is and to understand what a major sin is; and this is so that you can be conscious of it and keep away as the speaker of these lines said:

> **"Learn about evil, not with evil intent, but to be aware of it and avoid it, for verily, the one who does not know about evil will fall into it."**

Many people fall into matters which is clear *Shirk* and disbelief due to absolute ignorance about the Religion of Allāh (تَبَارَكَوَتَعَالَى); many have fallen into innovations and affairs contradictory to the *Sunnah* of the Prophet (صَلَّىٱللَّهُعَلَيْهِوَسَلَّمَ) due to their ignorance of the Religion of Allāh; like this is the case with sins and evil deeds—a majority of it is caused by ignorance in the Religion of Allāh. Hence, the first thing that is required from a person in the religion is to seek knowledge (of the religion) so that he knows his religion so that he knows the truth and so that he knows the guidance. This is why knowledge is given precedence over speech and action as Allāh (تَبَارَكَوَتَعَالَى) has said:

$$﴿ فَٱعْلَمْ أَنَّهُ لَا إِلَـٰهَ إِلَّا ٱللَّهُ وَٱسْتَغْفِرْ لِذَنۢبِكَ وَلِلْمُؤْمِنِينَ وَٱلْمُؤْمِنَـٰتِ ﴾$$

"So, <u>know</u> (O Muḥammad (صَلَّىٱللَّهُعَلَيْهِوَسَلَّمَ)) that Lā ilāha ill-allāh (none has the right to be worshipped but Allāh), and ask forgiveness for your sin, and also for (the sin of) believing men and believing women." [Sūrah Muḥammad (47):19]

Imām Bukhārī (رَحِمَهُٱللَّهُ) said: He (Allāh) started with knowledge before speech and action.

It is required of you to have knowledge of these three obstacles—*Shirk*, innovation, and sin—so that you are cautious of them and avoid them; and so that you warn your children and those under your care from falling into them:

And (remember) when Luqmān said to his son while advising him:

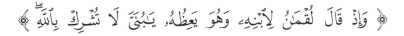

﴿ وَإِذْ قَالَ لُقْمَنُ لِٱبْنِهِۦ وَهُوَ يَعِظُهُۥ يَٰبُنَىَّ لَا تُشْرِكْ بِٱللَّهِ ﴾

"O, my son! Join not in worship others with Allāh." [Sūrah Luqmān (31):13]

Suppose that you one day say to your son: "O my son do not associate partners with Allāh in worship." And your son responds: "What is this *Shirk* that Allāh has forbidden us from committing?" Is it appropriate for you in this situation to not know what *Shirk* is? The reality of this affair is grave, and it is a must [that you be prepared]

And most commonly, the cause for many people falling into *Shirk* is ignorance, especially, with the increasing doubts overtaking the ignorant—and consequently, they turn them away from the Religion of Allāh (تَبَارَكَ وَتَعَالَى). Is it not a grave calamity and a severe catastrophe to a find a person ascribing himself to Islām raising his hands—in a way that they are only to be raised for Allāh—and stretching them out and after that invoking: "Support me O so and so? Assist me O so and so, catch me O so and so, get to me O so and so?" Subhānal-lāh! Where is Allāh [in their supplication]? Where is [their] *Tawhīd*? Where is their disassociating themselves from *Shirk*? What other cause is there for the likes of these people falling into these acts of *Shirk*—may Allāh protect you and us—than ignorance in the religion of Allāh and them being overcome with the doubts of the misguiding ones? Indeed, the Prophet (صَلَّى ٱللَّهُ عَلَيْهِ وَسَلَّمَ) has said:

إِنَّ أَخْوَفَ مَا أَخَافُ عَلَيْكُمُ الْأُمَّةَ الْمُضِلُّون

"The thing I fear most for you is the misguiding leaders."[38]

What do the "misguiding leaders" do? They beautify the falsehood and dress it up for the people; they dress up the misguidance under the clothes of guidance, and as a result, the people go astray and fall into different kinds of *Shirk* and innovations and become lost. So, it is a must that a person is extremely cautious. Are we ignorant about *Shirk*, which is the most dangerous and gravest of sins? Clarifying its danger, Allāh (سُبْحَانَهُوَتَعَالَى) said:

$$ ﴿ إِنَّ ٱللَّهَ لَا يَغْفِرُ أَن يُشْرَكَ بِهِۦ وَيَغْفِرُ مَا دُونَ ذَٰلِكَ لِمَن يَشَآءُ ﴾ $$

"Verily, Allāh forgives not that partners should be set up with Him (in worship), but He forgives except that (anything else) to whom He wills." [Sūrah an-Nisā (4):48]

And He (سُبْحَانَهُوَتَعَالَى) said:

$$ ﴿ إِنَّهُۥ مَن يُشْرِكْ بِٱللَّهِ فَقَدْ حَرَّمَ ٱللَّهُ عَلَيْهِ ٱلْجَنَّةَ وَمَأْوَىٰهُ ٱلنَّارُ وَمَا لِلظَّٰلِمِينَ مِنْ أَنصَارٍ ۝ ﴾ $$

---

[38] Reported by Ahmad (6/441) and authenticated by al-Albānī (رَحِمَهُٱللَّه) in *Sahīh al-Jāmi'* (1551)

"Verily, whosoever sets up partners (in worship) with
Allāh. Allāh has forbidden Paradise to him, and the Fire
will be his abode. And for the Zālimūn (polytheists and
wrong-doers) there are no helpers." [Sūrah al-Mā'idah
(5):72]

And He (سُبْحَانَهُوَتَعَالَى) said:

﴿ وَلَقَدۡ أُوحِىَ إِلَيۡكَ وَإِلَى ٱلَّذِينَ مِن قَبۡلِكَ لَئِنۡ أَشۡرَكۡتَ
لَيَحۡبَطَنَّ عَمَلُكَ وَلَتَكُونَنَّ مِنَ ٱلۡخَٰسِرِينَ ﴿٦٥﴾ بَلِ ٱللَّهَ
فَٱعۡبُدۡ وَكُن مِّنَ ٱلشَّٰكِرِينَ ﴿٦٦﴾ وَمَا قَدَرُوا۟ ٱللَّهَ حَقَّ قَدۡرِهِۦ
وَٱلۡأَرۡضُ جَمِيعًا قَبۡضَتُهُۥ يَوۡمَ ٱلۡقِيَٰمَةِ وَٱلسَّمَٰوَٰتُ مَطۡوِيَّٰتُۢ
بِيَمِينِهِۦ سُبۡحَٰنَهُۥ وَتَعَٰلَىٰ عَمَّا يُشۡرِكُونَ ﴿٦٧﴾ ﴾

"And indeed it has been revealed to you (O Muḥammad
صَلَّى ٱللَّهُ عَلَيۡهِ وَسَلَّمَ), as it was to those (Allāh's Messengers) before
you: "If you join others in worship with Allāh, (then)
surely (all) your deeds will be in vain, and you will
certainly be among the losers." Nay! But worship Allāh
(Alone and no one else), and be among the grateful. They
made not a just estimate of Allāh, such as is due to Him.
On the Day of Resurrection, the whole of the earth will be
grasped by His Hand, and the heavens will be rolled up in
His Right Hand. Glorified is He, and High is He above all

that they associate as partners with Him!" [Sūrah az-Zumar (39):65-67]

Has the one who appeals to other than Allāh for help and support (that only Allāh can provide)—or the one who invokes other than Allāh, or the one who requests relief from his distress and removal of his misfortunes from other than Allāh—justly estimated Allāh?! He (سُبْحَانَهُوَتَعَالَى) said:

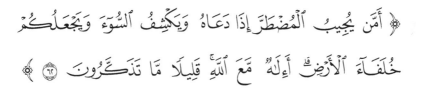

"Is not He (better than your gods) Who responds to the distressed one, when he calls on Him, and Who removes the evil, and makes you inheritors of the earth, generations after generations? Is there any ilāh (god) with Allāh? Little is that you remember!" [Sūrah an-Naml (27):62]

Meaning: Little do you remember and think; if you remembered, pondered, and reflected over the matter, you would not have fallen into that.

Indeed, *Shirk* (polytheism) is the most dangerous of affairs and the most unjust, and there is no injustice higher than it; thus, Allāh said:

$$﴿ إِنَّ ٱلشِّرْكَ لَظُلْمٌ عَظِيمٌ ۝ ﴾$$

"Verily! Joining others in worship with Allāh is a great Zūlm (wrong) indeed." [Sūrah Luqmān (31):13]

And what wrong is more grave than directing worship and supplication to other than the Creator (Allāh)?! He is the Creator, He is the Provider, He is the One Who Blesses, He is the One Who Bestows Favor; yet other than Him will be called upon, other than him will be invoked?!

On the authority of 'Abdullāh Ibn Mas'ūd (ﷺ) who said:

سَأَلْتُ النَّبِيَّ صَلَّى اللهُ عَلَيْهِ وَسَلَّمَ أَيُّ ذَنْبٍ أَعْظَمُ عِنْدَ اللهِ؟ قَالَ: أَنْ تَجْعَلَ للهِ نِدًّا وَهُوَ خَلَقَكَ

"I asked the Prophet (ﷺ): Which sin is the greatest with Allāh? He said: 'That you set up a rival with Allāh though He Alone created you.'"[39]

Meaning: The fact that He Alone exclusively created you and brought you into existence from nothing suffices in proving the obligation to single Him out alone in worship: so none should be invoked except Him, none should be asked except Him, none should be appealed to for aid and support except Him, and none should be set up as a rival or associate with Him—not a close angel or a sent Prophet or a saint or other than him—because worship is a right of the Creator (تَبَارَكَ وَتَعَالَى). Allāh (عَزَّوَجَلَّ) said:

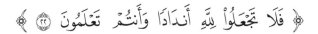

﴿ فَلَا تَجْعَلُواْ لِلَّهِ أَندَادًا وَأَنتُمْ تَعْلَمُونَ ۝ ﴾

---

[39] Reported by al-Bukhārī (4477) and Muslim (86)

"Then do not set up rivals unto Allāh (in worship) while you know (that He Alone has the right to be worshipped)." [Sūrah al-Baqarah (2):22]

"…While you know," meaning, while you know that you have no other Creator besides Allāh.

1. Who are the people of this Straight Path?

The favored people of the Path are those mentioned in Allāh's (سُبْحَانَهُ وَتَعَالَى) statement:

$$﴿ وَمَن يُطِعِ ٱللَّهَ وَٱلرَّسُولَ فَأُوْلَٰٓئِكَ مَعَ ٱلَّذِينَ أَنْعَمَ ٱللَّهُ عَلَيْهِم مِّنَ ٱلنَّبِيِّـۧنَ وَٱلصِّدِّيقِينَ وَٱلشُّهَدَآءِ وَٱلصَّٰلِحِينَ ﴾$$

"And whoso obeys Allāh and the Messenger (Muḥammad صَلَّى ٱللَّهُ عَلَيْهِ وَسَلَّمَ). They will be in the company of those on whom Allāh has bestowed His Grace, of the Prophets, the Siddiqūn (those followers of the Prophets who were first and foremost to believe in them, like Abu Bakr As-Siddiq رضي الله عنه), the martyrs, and the righteous. And how excellent these companions are!" [Sūrah an-Nisā (4):69]

And if you are from those whom Allāh favors with the treading of this Path, then do not feel alienated even if you are by yourself, because you are upon a path that was taken by the Prophets, the Siddīqūn, the martyrs and the righteous.

And His statement: "**…Those on whom You have bestowed Your Grace**" [Sūrah al-Fātihah (1):6], this shows that the treading of the Straight Path by a servant is a favor from Allāh; were it not for the favor of Allāh upon His servant to take the Straight Path, he would not be proceeding upon it—it is indeed from the Grace of Allāh. And a servant will not be from those upon whom Allāh bestows His Grace except with two matters: Knowledge of the truth and implementation of it; a knowledge that will guide the servant and righteous good deeds that will elevate the servant.

If beneficial knowledge is learned, then implementation of it is a must. If beneficial knowledge and righteous good deeds are both present, then the servant will be from those who will go along the Straight Path of Allāh. So, there are three types of people: a favored group [with the Grace of Allāh], a group who earned the wrath [of Allāh], and a group who is misguided and lost.

The favored group is the one who is favored by Allāh with beneficial knowledge and righteous good. The group that earned the anger is the one that has knowledge but does not act upon it, and this is a deviation in their knowledge and intentions. As for the other group, those who are misguided, they perform deeds without knowledge. They have their own knowledge and deeds with them, but they are all misguidance and innovations; Allāh said:

"Say (O Muḥammad ﷺ): "Shall We tell you the greatest losers in respect of (their) deeds? Those whose efforts have been wasted in this life while they thought that they were acquiring good by their deeds!" (al-Kahf (18): 103-104]

Through this, you should know yourself and your urgent need to be from those whom Allāh favors with taking His Straight Path. How splendid is it for the believer to be conscious of how great and dire his need is to be traversing along this Path, to remain firm upon it until he meets Allāh (عَزَّوَجَلَّ) who will be pleased with Him? This is the greatest blessing, the most splendid favor, and the grandest gift period! For this reason, Allāh (سُبْحَانَهُوَتَعَالَى) said:

"The Way of those on whom You have bestowed Your Grace." [Sūrah al-Fātihah (1):6]

So, the greatest blessing, most majestic favor, and the grandest gift is that Allāh (جَلَّوَعَلَا) guides you to the Straight Path, keeps you steadfast upon it until you meet Him (سُبْحَانَهُوَتَعَالَى) while He is pleased with you.

Thus, in this blessed context, it becomes clear that the Path is straight, it mentions who are its favored people are, and who are the ones that deviated from it.

5ᵀᴴ GUIDELINE: A WARNING AGAINST DEVIATING FROM THE PATH OF ALLĀH

It is incumbent to know that Satan is persistently diligent in averting the servant from the Straight Path of Allāh in one of two ways: through doubts or desires. Through doubts, a person will innovate in the religion. Through desires, a person will fall into sins and criminal matters. Satan deceives a person, plots against him, and plans to ward him off [from the Straight Path]. He carefully analyzes the state of a person and his inclinations and the best way to cause him to deviate: either through doubts or desires.

As some of the *Salaf* said: "Satan is the '*Yash-Shām*' of the hearts," meaning, he looks at what the human is inclined to; if he finds him adherent to and diligent in the religion, he will strive in expelling him from the religion through doubts. He will persist in trying to belittle his religiosity, having *Taqwaa* and worship. Thus, the person will begin to overexert himself more than others until he strays from the Straight Path. As for the one whose faith is weak, Satan will come to him through desires. So, deviance from the Straight Path of Allāh occurs either through doubts or desires.

If a person strays from the Straight Path by way of doubts, then this is evidence of one's knowledge having errors. If it occurs by way of desires, then this is evidence of faultiness in the deeds. And the Religion of Allāh (تَبَارَكَ وَتَعَالَى)—which is the Straight Path of Allāh— is a rectification for knowledge and deeds. Allāh (سُبْحَانَهُ وَتَعَالَى) said:

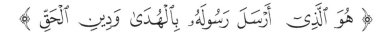

﴿ هُوَ ٱلَّذِىٓ أَرْسَلَ رَسُولَهُۥ بِٱلْهُدَىٰ وَدِينِ ٱلْحَقِّ ﴾

"It is He Who has sent His Messenger (Muḥammad ﷺ) with guidance and the religion of truth (Islām), to make it superior over all religions." [Sūrah at-Tawbah (9):33]

The scholars say that this means "with beneficial knowledge and righteous deeds." If these two are actualized, the servant will successfully be traveling along the Straight Path of Allāh. And the Prophet (ﷺ) use to say after completing the morning *Salāh*:

اللَّهُمَّ إِنِّي أَسْأَلُكَ عِلْمًا نَافِعًا وَرِزْقًا طَيِّبًا وَعَمَلاً مُتَقَبَّلاً

"O Allāh, I ask You for beneficial knowledge, goodly provision, and acceptable deeds."[40]

Beneficial knowledge will cause a person to be guided to the path of goodness. Righteous deeds will cause a person to traverse along the path of goodness with dignity and loftiness. Still, Satan wants the servant to go astray either through faultiness in his knowledge or in his deeds. If a person's knowledge becomes faulty, then he will be lost and misguided; and if his deeds become corrupt, he will be from those who earned the wrath [of Allāh]. Thus, Allāh said in the conclusion of the *Sūrah*:

---

[40] Reported by Ibn Mājah (925) and authenticated by al-Albānī (رحمه الله) in *Sahīh Ibn Mājah* (762)

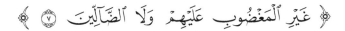

"...Not (the way) of those who earned Your Anger (such as the Jews), nor of those who went astray (such as the Christians)." [Sūrah al-Fātihah (1):7]

Those who earned the anger became corrupt in their deeds, and those who went astray became corrupt in their knowledge. Hence, a person will not be safe from the anger, the wrath, and the punishment of Allāh unless he becomes guided to the Straight Path and is steadfast upon it and does not stray from it due to doubts or desires.

And the subject of desires is a dangerous one for people; many people exit from the Straight Path of Allāh because of it—following their whims and the callers to lusts that are always competing with each other in deterring the people from goodness and causing them to fall into lewdness and impermissible matters through numerous magazines: through satellite channels, the internet, the baseless magazines, and many other means.

And on this note, listen attentively to the following statement of Allāh (سُبْحَانَهُوَتَعَالَى) and ponder over it:

﴿ وَٱللَّهُ يُرِيدُ أَن يَتُوبَ عَلَيۡكُمۡ وَيُرِيدُ ٱلَّذِينَ يَتَّبِعُونَ ٱلشَّهَوَٰتِ أَن تَمِيلُواْ مَيۡلًا عَظِيمًا ۝ ﴾

"Allāh wishes to accept your repentance, but those who follow their lusts, wish that you (believers) should deviate

tremendously away (from the Right Path).” [Sūrah an-Nisā (4):27]

Meaning: they wish that you deviate from Allāh's Straight Path and the upright way. There is a group of people who follow their lusts and want others to likewise actively become inclined to their desires just as they did; so that their wickedness is not exclusive to only them. 'Uthmān Ibn 'Affān (رضي الله عنه) said: "The adulteress wishes that all the women fornicate," this is because when a person falls into the traps of lusts and becomes polluted with it, he does not want to be the only one in his community in this regard; instead, he wants others to be upon his way. Thus, he energetically works to misguide the safe ones and drag them to a path of desires. From this—especially in our time—is their specialization in presenting the different types of lusts and entrapping the people [through them] and taking their wealth and causing them to fall into the traps of unlawful desires and false pleasures which Allāh (تَبَارَكَوَتَعَالَى) has forbidden for His servants and cautioned them against.

Therefore, it is mandatory upon the servant to be cautious from sinning and evil deeds and falling into that which will anger the Magnificent Lord (جَلَّجَلَالُهُ). And this blessed *Sūrah* encourages you (by the will of Allāh (جَلَّوَعَلَا)) to abstain from these vices, as Allāh (عَزَّوَجَلَّ) said:

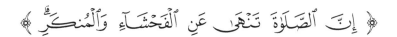

﴿ إِنَّ ٱلصَّلَوٰةَ تَنۡهَىٰ عَنِ ٱلۡفَحۡشَآءِ وَٱلۡمُنكَرِ ﴾

"Verily, *as-Salāh* (the prayer) prevents from *al-Fahshā'* (i.e., great sins of every kind, unlawful sexual intercourse)

and al-Munkar (i.e., disbelief, polytheism, and every kind of evil, wicked deed).” [Sūrah al-’Ankabūt (29):45]

The most significant pillar of the *Salāh* is *al-Fātihah* as has been affirmed in the *Hadīth Qudsī*:

قَسَمْتُ الصَّلَاةَ بَيْنِي وَبَيْنَ عَبْدِي نِصْفَيْنِ

“The *Salāh* is divided into two halves between My servant and Me. Half of it is for Me, and the other half is for My servant.”[41]

He called *al-Fātihah* a *Salāh*. However, the prayer that “prevents from *al-Fahshā’* and *al-Munkar*” is the one in which a person reflects and ponders over the Words of Allāh (عَزَّوَجَلَّ), especially this great *Sūrah* which is an essential pillar from the pillars of the prayer. Indeed, it guides the servant, by the will of Allāh (تَبَارَكَوَتَعَالَى), to the Straight Path of Allāh.

If a believer recites, **“Guide us to the Straight Path”** (al-Fātihah: 5) every day and ponders over it, then if his soul speaks to him about straying from it (i.e., the Path) through desires, pleasures or impermissible acts, he will refrain from doing so and strive against his soul and work diligently to hold it back and restrain it from entering that which Allāh (عَزَّوَجَلَّ) has forbidden or deviating from

---

[41] Reported by Muslim (395)

Allāh's Straight Path as an implementation of the statement of Allāh (تَبَارَكَ وَتَعَالَى):

$$﴿ وَٱلَّذِينَ جَٰهَدُواْ فِينَا لَنَهْدِيَنَّهُمْ سُبُلَنَا وَإِنَّ ٱللَّهَ لَمَعَ ٱلْمُحْسِنِينَ ۝ ﴾$$

"As for those who strive hard in Us (Our Cause), We will surely guide them to Our Paths (i.e., Allāh's religion - Islāmic Monotheism). And verily, Allāh is with the *Muhsinūn* (good-doers)." [Sūrah al-'Ankabūt (29):69]

The sins that Allāh has forbidden His servants from committing are two types: Major and minor sins. Allāh (سُبْحَانَهُ وَتَعَالَى) said:

$$﴿ وَكُلُّ صَغِيرٍ وَكَبِيرٍ مُّسْتَطَرٌ ۝ ﴾$$

"And everything, small and big, is written down (in al-Lawh al-Mahfūz)." [Sūrah al-Qamar (54): 53]

Meaning: It is written against the servant, and he will find it on the scales of his bad deeds on the Day of Judgment. For this reason, Allāh (جَلَّ وَعَلَا) said in another verse:

وَيَقُولُونَ يَٰوَيْلَتَنَا مَالِ هَٰذَا ٱلْكِتَٰبِ لَا يُغَادِرُ صَغِيرَةً وَلَا
كَبِيرَةً إِلَّآ أَحْصَىٰهَا وَوَجَدُوا۟ مَا عَمِلُوا۟ حَاضِرًا وَلَا يَظْلِمُ رَبُّكَ
أَحَدًا ۝

**"And the Book (one's Record) will be placed (in the right
hand for a believer in the Oneness of Allāh, and in the left
hand for a disbeliever in the Oneness of Allāh). You will
see the Mujrimūn (criminals, polytheists, sinners), fearful
of that which is (recorded) therein. They will say: "Woe to
us! What sort of Book is this that leaves neither a small
thing nor a big thing, but has recorded it with numbers!"
And they will find all that they did, placed before them,
and your Lord treats no one with injustice." [Sūrah al-
Kahf (18):49]**

Allāh (جَلَّوَعَلَا) keeps account of all of that, just as He (سُبْحَانَهُوَتَعَالَى) said:

أَحْصَىٰهُ ٱللَّهُ وَنَسُوهُ

**"Allāh has kept account of it, while they have forgotten it."
[Sūrah al-Mujādilah (58):6]**

The pleasure found in impermissible acts vanishes and finishes in
its time; however, what does remain is its ill consequence, as was
said:

"The pleasures of the unlawful acts will vanish for the one who experienced them at their peak; however, the sin and shame will remain; the ill consequences will remain. There is no good in a pleasure that is followed by the Fire [of Hell]."[42]

One of the *Salaf* said: "When I commit a sin, I see its effects in the behavior of my wife and my riding beast."[43] And this is from its ill effects in this world, as for the Hereafter, they are intense and more perilous. Allāh (عَزَّوَجَلَّ) has commended His believing servants for abstaining from major sins and not committing them in many verses in His Book, such as His statement (سبحانه):

﴿ ٱلَّذِينَ يَجْتَنِبُونَ كَبَـٰٓئِرَ ٱلْإِثْمِ وَٱلْفَوَٰحِشَ إِلَّا ٱللَّمَمَ إِنَّ رَبَّكَ وَٰسِعُ ٱلْمَغْفِرَةِ ﴾

"Those who avoid great sins and *al-Fawāhish* (illegal sexual intercourse) except the small faults, your Lord is of vast forgiveness." [Sūrah an-Najm (53):32]

And His statement (تَبَارَكَوَتَعَالَى):

---

[42] Mentioned by Imām 'Abdur-Rahmān Ibn Muhammad Ibn 'Abdur-Rahmān al-'Ulaymī al-Maqdisī in his book, *al-Manhaj al-Ahmad Fī Tarājim Ashāb al-Imām Ahmad* (1/94)

[43] From the speech of al-Fudayl Ibn 'Iyād (رَحِمَهُٱللَّه) and his wording in *Hilyah al-Awliyā* (8/109) is: "...I would know it in the behavior of my donkey and my servant." Look in the book *ad-Dā wad-Dawā* by Ibn al-Qayyim (134)

$$\left\{ \text{وَٱلَّذِينَ يَجْتَنِبُونَ كَبَـٰٓئِرَ ٱلْإِثْمِ وَٱلْفَوَٰحِشَ وَإِذَا مَا غَضِبُواْ هُمْ يَغْفِرُونَ} \text{ (٣٧)} \right\}$$

"And those who avoid the greater sins, and *al-Fawāhish*
(illegal sexual intercourse), and when they are angry,
forgive." [Sūrah ash-Shūrā (42):37]

And His statement (تَبَارَكَ وَتَعَالَى):

$$\left\{ \text{إِن تَجْتَنِبُواْ كَبَـٰٓئِرَ مَا تُنْهَوْنَ عَنْهُ نُكَفِّرْ عَنكُمْ سَيِّئَاتِكُمْ وَنُدْخِلْكُم مُّدْخَلًا كَرِيمًا} \text{ (٣١)} \right\}$$

"If you avoid the great sins which you are forbidden to do,
We shall expiate from you your (small) sins, and admit you
to a Noble Entrance (i.e., Paradise)." [Sūrah an-Nisā
(4):31]

So the Muslim traveling along the Straight Path of Allāh needs to
acquire knowledge and be acquainted with the major sins to be
cautious of them; so he should know about the major sins and the
associated punishments for the one who commits them, as well as
the verses and *Ahādīth* (Prophetic sayings) that warn against them.
Indeed, this knowledge—by the will of Allāh (عَزَّوَجَلَّ)—will direct
you on how to avoid them. And books concerning this topic are
many, and from the best of them is the book, *al-Kabā'ir (The Major
Sins)*, by Imām adh-Dhahabī (رَحِمَهُ ٱللَّهُ). Indeed, he did an excellent job

and benefited [others]; he presented the major sins and added extremely precious commentary that every Muslim needs.

He (رَحِمَهُٱللَّهُ) mentioned in his book the statement of Ibn 'Abbās (رَضِيَٱللَّهُعَنْهُمَا) when he was asked about the number of the major sins: "Are they seven?" He (ﷺ) said: "They are closer to seventy."[44] And Imām adh-Dhahabī (رَحِمَهُٱللَّهُ) said: "By Allāh Ibn 'Abbās spoke the truth…"[45] This is because the matters that Allāh (عَزَّوَجَلَّ) has forbidden for His servants and threatened them about committing them are many; they are not seven or ten or twenty. He (the author) then began listing more than seventy major sins in his book, *al-Kabā'ir*. And he mentions with every major sin its proofs from the Book of Allāh and the Sunnah of His Prophet (صَلَّىٱللَّهُعَلَيْهِوَعَلَىآلِهِوَسَلَّمَ). So what is compulsory upon you is to read this book in its entirety and become familiarized with these major sins to avoid them; and that you ask Allāh (جَلَّوَعَلَا) to protect you from falling into any of them so that you can be from those that traverse the Straight Path of Allāh without crookedness.

For this reason, it is a must that a person learns and seeks to understand; because from the fundamental aspects of taking Allāh's Straight Path is knowledge about the guidance so that you can implement it; knowledge about falsehood and criminal matters so that you can abstain from it. This is why the Prophet (عَلَيْهِٱلصَّلَاةُوَٱلسَّلَامُ)

---

[44] Reported by Ibn Jarīr at-Tabarī (6/651)
[45] Look in the book, *al-Kabā'ir*, by adh-Dhahabī, the *Tahqīq* of Mashūr Hasan Āli Salmān (89), the Maktabah al-Furqān edition, UAE

use to warn his nation from the major sins on many occasions, like his statement:

اجْتَنِبُوا السَّبْعَ الْمُوبِقَاتِ ". قَالُوا يَا رَسُولَ اللَّهِ وَمَا هُنَّ قَالَ " الشِّرْكُ بِاللَّهِ، وَالسِّحْرُ، وَقَتْلُ النَّفْسِ الَّتِي حَرَّمَ اللَّهُ إِلاَّ بِالْحَقِّ، وَأَكْلُ الرِّبَا، وَأَكْلُ مَالِ الْيَتِيمِ، وَالتَّوَلِّي يَوْمَ الزَّحْفِ، وَقَذْفُ الْمُحْصَنَاتِ الْمُؤْمِنَاتِ الْغَافِلَاتِ

"Avoid the seven destructive matters: Associating anyone or anything with Allāh in worship; practicing sorcery, killing of someone without a just cause whom Allāh has forbidden, devouring the property of an orphan, eating of usury, fleeing from the battlefield and slandering chaste believing women who never even thought about violating their chastity."[46]

And on the authority of Abī Bakrah (رضي الله عنه) who said that the Prophet (صَلَّى اللَّهُ عَلَيْهِ وَسَلَّمَ) said:

---

[46] Reported by al-Bukhārī (2766) and Muslim (89)

أَلاَ أُنَبِّئُكُمْ بِأَكْبَرِ الْكَبَائِرِ - ثَلاَثًا - الإِشْرَاكُ بِاللَّهِ وَعُقُوقُ الْوَالِدَيْنِ

وَشَهَادَةُ الزُّورِ أَوْ قَوْلُ الزُّورِ " . وَكَانَ رَسُولُ اللَّهِ صلى الله عليه وسلم

مُتَّكِئًا فَجَلَسَ فَمَازَالَ يُكَرِّرُهَا حَتَّى قُلْنَا لَيْتَهُ سَكَتَ

"'Should I not inform you about the most grievous of the grave sins?' He repeated it three times. They replied: 'Certainly, O Messenger of Allāh.' Then he said: 'Associating anyone with Allāh in worship, disobedience to parents, false testimony or false utterance.' The Prophet was reclining, then he sat up, and he repeated it so many times that we wished he would stop."[47]

And on the authority of Qays al-Ashja'ī (ﷺ) who said:

قَالَ رَسُولُ اللهِ صَلَّى اللهُ عَلَيْهِ وَسَلَّمَ فِي حَجَّةِ الْوَدَاعِ: أَلَا إِنَّمَا هُنَّ أَرْبَعٌ:

أَنْ لَا تُشْرِكُوا بِاللهِ شَيْئاً، وَلَا تَقْتُلُوا النَّفْسَ الَّتِي حَرَّمَ اللهُ إِلَّا بِالْحَقِّ،

وَلَا تَزْنُوا، وَلَا تَسْرِقُوا، قَالَ: فَمَا أَنَا بِأَشُحَّ عَلَيْهِنَّ مِنِّي، إِذْ سَمِعْتُهُنَّ مِنْ

رَسُولِ اللهِ صَلَّى اللهُ عَلَيْهِ وَسَلَّمَ

"The Messenger of Allāh (ﷺ) in the farewell _Hajj_ said: 'Verily, they are four: Do not associate anything with Allāh in worship, nor take a life which Allāh has made

---

[47] Reported by al-Bukhārī (2654) and Muslim (87)

prohibited without a just cause, nor commit unlawful intercourse, nor steal.' I have diligently and miserly held on to these words since I heard them from the Messenger of Allāh (ﷺ)."[48]

Look at this great advice. The Prophet (عَلَيْهِ وَعَلَى آلِهِ الصَّلَاةُ وَالسَّلَامُ) gave his Ummah sincere advice and clarified to them (matters), and directed and guided them to the straight path; just as Allāh (جَلَّ وَعَلَا) ordered him to do so:

$$﴿ وَإِنَّكَ لَتَهْدِىٓ إِلَىٰ صِرَٰطٍ مُّسْتَقِيمٍ ۝ صِرَٰطِ ٱللَّهِ ٱلَّذِى لَهُۥ مَا فِى ٱلسَّمَٰوَٰتِ وَمَا فِى ٱلْأَرْضِ أَلَآ إِلَى ٱللَّهِ تَصِيرُ ٱلْأُمُورُ ۝ ﴾$$

"We guide whosoever of Our slaves We will. And verily, you (O Muḥammad ﷺ) are indeed guiding (mankind) to the Straight Path (i.e., Allah's religion of Islamic Monotheism). The Path of Allah, to Whom belongs all that is in the heavens and all that is in the earth. Verily, all the matters at the end go to Allah (for decision)." [Sūrah ash-Shuʿrāʾ (42):52-53]

---

[48] Reported by Ahmad (4/339) and authenticated by al-Albānī (رَحِمَهُ ٱللَّهُ) in *as-Saḥīḥah* (1759)

As for the first three that he (ﷺ) mentioned, they are found in the statement of Allāh (جَلَّوَعَلَا) describing the servants of the Most Merciful:

﴿ وَٱلَّذِينَ لَا يَدۡعُونَ مَعَ ٱللَّهِ إِلَٰهًا ءَاخَرَ وَلَا يَقۡتُلُونَ ٱلنَّفۡسَ ٱلَّتِي حَرَّمَ ٱللَّهُ إِلَّا بِٱلۡحَقِّ وَلَا يَزۡنُونَۚ وَمَن يَفۡعَلۡ ذَٰلِكَ يَلۡقَ أَثَامًا ٦٨ يُضَٰعَفۡ لَهُ ٱلۡعَذَابُ يَوۡمَ ٱلۡقِيَٰمَةِ وَيَخۡلُدۡ فِيهِۦ مُهَانًا ٦٩ إِلَّا مَن تَابَ وَءَامَنَ وَعَمِلَ عَمَلًا صَٰلِحًا فَأُوْلَٰئِكَ يُبَدِّلُ ٱللَّهُ سَيِّـَٔاتِهِمۡ حَسَنَٰتٍۗ وَكَانَ ٱللَّهُ غَفُورًا رَّحِيمًا ٧٠ ﴾

"And those who invoke not any other ilāh (god) along with Allāh, nor kill such person Allāh has forbidden, except for just cause, nor commit illegal sexual intercourse - and whoever does this shall receive the punishment. The torment will be doubled to him on the Day of Resurrection, and he will abide therein in disgrace; Except those who repent and believe (in Islāmic Monotheism), and do righteous deeds, for those, Allāh will change their sins into good deeds, and Allāh is Oft-Forgiving, Most Merciful."
[Sūrah al-Furqān (25):68-70]

And how beautiful would it be for a person to hold himself to account in this world, the field for the performance of deeds, before Allāh (تَبَارَكَوَتَعَالَى) holds him to account on the Day of Judgment, in the field of recompense. 'Alī (رضي الله عنه) said: "This world has departed with its back turned and the Hereafter has advanced coming forward. And every one of them has children, so be from the children of the Hereafter and not the children of this world; for indeed, today is time for action and no accountability, and tomorrow is the time for accountability and no action."[49]

As sincere advice to this nation, the people of knowledge have clarified what distinguishes a major sin from the rest: If Allāh and His Messenger (صَلَّى ٱللَّهُ عَلَيْهِ وَسَلَّمَ) mention an issue and say that it is forbidden, then add that its doer will earn the wrath of Allāh, or that he will be cursed, or that the Fire of Hell will be prepared for him; then this is classified as a major sin. Also, if a prescribed punishment for it in this world is mentioned such as capital punishment, stoning, lashes or amputation of his hand and what is similar to these; as well as if he (the Prophet) (صَلَّى ٱللَّهُ عَلَيْهِ وَسَلَّمَ) says concerning a sin that, "he is not from me," then this similarly classifies an issue as a major sin.

adh-Dhahabī and other than him mention these rules in the writings that clarify major sins. If you understand this subject and are well acquainted with the major sins and their prescribed punishments and you realize that they are many, as well as familiarizing yourself with the texts that warn against the major sins; you will have attained knowledge in this field with which Allāh (تَبَارَكَ وَتَعَالَى) will protect you from committing these grievous and atrocious sins. Therefore, it is a must that a servant is diligent in [gaining knowledge] concerning this topic; so that he can traverse on the Straight Path of Allāh without deviating and swerving. And I ask Allāh to honor us all and

---

[49] Added as commentary by al-Bukhārī—in a way indicating that it is sound— before *Hadīth* # 6418.

you with being distant from what he made impermissible; and that He grants us success to fulfill what He has ordered.

If Allāh (جَلَّوَعَلَا) honors you with abstaining from these major sins, then look at the lofty promises and the honorable entrance that will be prepared for you, Allāh (عَزَّوَجَلَّ) said:

﴿ ٱلَّذِينَ يَجْتَنِبُونَ كَبَٰٓئِرَ ٱلْإِثْمِ وَٱلْفَوَٰحِشَ إِلَّا ٱللَّمَمَ إِنَّ رَبَّكَ وَٰسِعُ ٱلْمَغْفِرَةِ ﴾

"Those who avoid great sins and al-Fawāhish (illegal sexual intercourse) except the small faults, verily, your Lord is of vast forgiveness." [Sūrah an-Najm (53):32]

He tied the "vast forgiveness" to the avoidance of great sins. And he (تَبَارَكَوَتَعَالَى) said:

﴿ إِن تَجْتَنِبُواْ كَبَٰٓئِرَ مَا تُنْهَوْنَ عَنْهُ نُكَفِّرْ عَنكُمْ سَيِّئَاتِكُمْ وَنُدْخِلْكُم مُّدْخَلًا كَرِيمًا ٣١ ﴾

"If you avoid the great sins which you are forbidden to do, We shall expiate from you your (small) sins, and admit you to a Noble Entrance (i.e., Paradise)." [Sūrah an-Nisā (4):31]

It is said that the "Noble Entrance" is Paradise, and it also said that it means, every good and type of happiness that is obtained by the servant in this world and the next.

He (ﷺ) said:

الصَّلَوَاتُ الْخَمْسُ، وَالْجُمْعَةُ إِلَى الْجُمْعَةِ، وَرَمَضَانُ إِلَى رَمَضَانَ،
مُكَفِّرَاتٌ مَا بَيْنَهُنَّ، إِذَا اجْتَنَبَ الْكَبَائِرَ.

**"The five daily (prescribed) prayers, and Friday (prayer)
to the next Friday (prayer), and the fasting of *Ramaḍān* to
the next *Ramaḍān*, are expiation of the sins committed in
between them, so long as major sins are avoided."[50]**

It is a must to repent from a major sin; but as for the minor ones, the
good deeds wipe them away by the will of Allāh (جَلَّ وَعَلَا), as Allāh
(سُبْحَانَهُ وَتَعَالَى) said:

﴿ إِنَّ ٱلْحَسَنَٰتِ يُذْهِبْنَ ٱلسَّيِّئَاتِ ﴾

**Verily, the good deeds remove the evil deeds (i.e., small
sins). (Hūd: 114)**

And as the Prophet (ﷺ) said:

وَأَتْبِعِ السَّيِّئَةَ الْحَسَنَةَ تَمْحُهَا

---

[50] Reported by Muslim (233)

"Do good deeds after doing bad ones. The former will wipe out the latter."[51]

However, a good deed does not wipe away a major sin, because a major sin requires that you repent from it.

On the authority of Sa'īd (رضي الله عنه) who said: "The Messenger of Allāh (صَلَّى اللَّهُ عَلَيْهِ وَسَلَّمَ) said:

أَمَّا أَهْلُ النَّارِ الَّذِينَ هُمْ أَهْلُهَا فَإِنَّهُمْ لاَ يَمُوتُونَ فِيهَا وَلاَ يَحْيَوْنَ وَلَكِنْ نَاسٌ أَصَابَتْهُمُ النَّارُ بِذُنُوبِهِمْ - أَوْ قَالَ بِخَطَايَاهُمْ - فَأَمَاتَهُمْ إِمَاتَةً حَتَّى إِذَا كَانُوا فَحْمًا أُذِنَ بِالشَّفَاعَةِ فَجِيءَ بِهِمْ ضَبَائِرَ ضَبَائِرَ فَبُثُّوا عَلَى أَنْهَارِ الْجَنَّةِ ثُمَّ قِيلَ يَا أَهْلَ الْجَنَّةِ أَفِيضُوا عَلَيْهِمْ . فَيَنْبُتُونَ نَبَاتَ الْحِبَّةِ تَكُونُ فِي حَمِيلِ السَّيْلِ

'The (permanent) inhabitants of the Fire are those who are doomed to it, and verily they would neither die nor live in it. But the people whom the Fire would afflict (temporarily) on account of their sins,' or he (the narrator) said: on account of their misdeeds. 'He would cause them to die till they would be turned into charcoal. Then they would be granted intercession and would be brought in groups and would be spread on the rivers of Paradise and

---

[51] Reported by at-Tirmidhī (1987) and graded *Hasan* by al-Albānī (رحمه الله) in *Sahīh Sunan at-Tirmidhī* (2/373)

then it would be said: 'O inhabitants of Paradise, pour water over them;' then they would sprout forth like the sprouting of seed in the silt carried by flood.' A man among the people said: '(It appears) as if the Messenger of Allāh (ﷺ) lived in the desert.'"[52]

This will be the state of the people who commit major sins, such as fornication, robbery, disobedience to parents, lying, cheating, backbiting, and slandering. Is it not befitting for us while we are alive to consider, know, and avoid these major sins, and to ask our Lord (جَلَّ وَعَلَا) to distance us from them? And [is it not also befitting for us] to not continue living in this life pretending to be heedless and negligent as if this matter does not concern us until one of us suddenly reaches the end of his appointed time and meets Allāh with these sins and heinous offenses? Thus, it is mandatory upon the Muslim to advise himself, fear his Lord, and refrain from what He (تَبَارَكَ وَتَعَالَى) has made unlawful for him.

[But bear in mind that] no matter what kind of sin or how many sins you commit, verily, Allāh (عَزَّوَجَلَّ) accepts the repentance of the one who repents to him. Hence, it is not permissible for anyone amongst us to despair in the mercy of Allāh or loses hope in the clemency of Allāh; rather, a person should rush to repent and turn back to Allāh (عَزَّوَجَلَّ); and Allāh forgives the sin of the one who repents no matter how great it is. And consider this blessed call in the Magnificent *Qur'ān*:

---

[52] Reported by Muslim (185)

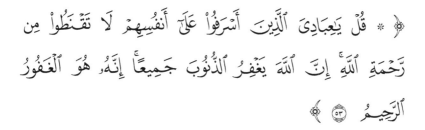

"Say: "O ʿIbādī (My slaves) who have transgressed against themselves (by committing evil deeds and sins)! Despair not of the Mercy of Allāh, verily Allāh forgives all sins. Truly, He is Oft-Forgiving, Most Merciful." [Sūrah az-Zumar (39):53]

So, from the good things that are befitting for a person to do is advice himself, fear Allāh (جَلَّ وَعَلَا) and strive against himself in repenting from all his bad deeds:

﴿ وَٱلَّذِينَ جَٰهَدُواْ فِينَا لَنَهْدِيَنَّهُمْ سُبُلَنَا وَإِنَّ ٱللَّهَ لَمَعَ ٱلْمُحْسِنِينَ ۞ ٦٩ ﴾

"As for those who strive hard in Us (Our Cause), We will surely guide them to Our Paths (i.e., Allāh's religion - Islāmic Monotheism). And verily, Allāh is with the *Muhsinūn* (good-doers)." [Sūrah al-ʾAnkabūt (29):69]

Another matter concerning repentance is that it shows us the greatness of the generosity and kindness of our Lord (سُبْحَانَهُ وَتَعَالَى) even though the obedience of the obedient ones does not benefit Him and nor does the disobedience of the sinners harm Him; He (سُبْحَانَهُوَتَعَالَى) said:

$$ ﴿ مَّنِ ٱهۡتَدَىٰ فَإِنَّمَا يَهۡتَدِى لِنَفۡسِهِۦ وَمَن ضَلَّ فَإِنَّمَا يَضِلُّ عَلَيۡهَا ﴾ $$

"Whoever goes right, then he goes right only for the benefit of his own self. And whoever goes astray, then he goes astray to his own loss." [Sūrah al-Isrā (17):15]

And Allāh (سُبْحَانَهُوَتَعَالَى) says in the *Hadīth Qudsī*:

يَا عِبَادِي لَوْ أَنَّ أَوَّلَكُمْ وَآخِرَكُمْ وَإِنْسَكُمْ وَجِنَّكُمْ كَانُوا عَلَى أَتْقَى قَلْبِ رَجُلٍ وَاحِدٍ مِنْكُمْ مَا زَادَ ذَلِكَ فِي مُلْكِي شَيْئًا يَا عِبَادِي لَوْ أَنَّ أَوَّلَكُمْ وَآخِرَكُمْ وَإِنْسَكُمْ وَجِنَّكُمْ كَانُوا عَلَى أَفْجَرِ قَلْبِ رَجُلٍ وَاحِدٍ مَا نَقَصَ ذَلِكَ مِنْ مُلْكِي شَيْئًا

"O My servants, even if the first amongst you and the last amongst you and even the whole of the human race of yours, and that of the Jinns, become (equal in) God-conscious like the heart of a single person amongst you, nothing of that would add to My Kingdom. O My servants, even if the first amongst you and the last amongst you and the whole human race of yours and that of the Jinns too in unison become the most wicked (all beating) like the heart

of a single person, it would cause no loss to My Kingdom."[53]

And notice Allāh's generosity and tremendous kindness with regards to the one repenting; the Prophet (عَلَيْهِ ٱلصَّلَاةُ وَٱلسَّلَامُ) said:

لَلَّهُ أَشَدُّ فَرَحًا بِتَوْبَةِ عَبْدِهِ حِينَ يَتُوبُ إِلَيْهِ مِنْ أَحَدِكُمْ كَانَ عَلَى رَاحِلَتِهِ بِأَرْضِ فَلَاةٍ فَانْفَلَتَتْ مِنْهُ وَعَلَيْهَا طَعَامُهُ وَشَرَابُهُ فَأَيِسَ مِنْهَا فَأَتَى شَجَرَةً فَاضْطَجَعَ فِي ظِلِّهَا قَدْ أَيِسَ مِنْ رَاحِلَتِهِ فَبَيْنَا هُوَ كَذَلِكَ إِذَا هُوَ بِهَا قَائِمَةً عِنْدَهُ فَأَخَذَ بِخِطَامِهَا ثُمَّ قَالَ مِنْ شِدَّةِ الْفَرَحِ اللَّهُمَّ أَنْتَ عَبْدِي وَأَنَا رَبُّكَ أَخْطَأَ مِنْ شِدَّةِ الْفَرَحِ.

"Verily, Allāh is more pleased with the repentance of His slave than a person riding his camel that is carrying his provision of food and drink in a waterless desert and then loses it (the camel). He, having lost all hope (to get it back), comes to a tree and lies down in its shade, disheartened about his camel; when all of a sudden, he finds the camel standing before him. He takes hold of its reins and then out of boundless joy blurts out: 'O Allāh, You are my slave and I am Your lord.' He commits this mistake out of extreme joy."[54]

---

[53] Reported by Muslim (2577)
[54] Reported by Muslim (2747)

Allāh (عَزَّوَجَلَّ) is pleased with the penitence of those that repent, and
He loves for them to repent; He sent the messengers and ordered the
people of knowledge and the propagators [of the religion] in His
book to direct and call the people to repent. The door of repentance
is open to human beings and will not close until one of the following
two matters occur: If a person's soul comes to his throat (to exit) and
he witnesses death—because the repentance of the one who
witnesses death was like that of Pharaoh when he was about to
drown—his repentance will be rejected; and if the sun rises from the
west (a prophesized sign from the signs preceding the Day of
Judgment), repentance will also not be accepted; because when the
people witness this, all of them will believe in it and repentance at
this time will be of no benefit. So the repentance that is done before
these two circumstances is the beneficial one.

Thus, it is compulsory upon every single one of us to sincerely
advise himself and turn to Allāh (عَزَّوَجَلَّ) in repentance; and be
devoted to adhering to this Straight Path.

In summary, from the fundamental aspects of clinging to the
Straight Path is being cautious from the major sins and this entails
several matters: having knowledge about the major sins and being
well acquainted with them, striving against oneself in withholding
from them, being cautious of falling into them and repenting from
what has occurred (i.e., of previous sins). Above all of these:
Seeking assistance from Allāh (تَبَارَكَوَتَعَالَى) in being protected from
committing them and being steadfast upon righteousness.

6TH GUIDELINE: THE ESTABLISHMENT OF ĪMĀN (FAITH) IN THE LAST DAY

From the directives of this blessed *Sūrah* is the affirmation of *Īmān* in the Last Day (the Day of Resurrection), that great day in which the people will stand in front of the Lord of all that exists (جَلَّ وَعَلَا) so that He can compensate them according to what they put forth from deeds in this world:

﴿ لِيَجۡزِيَ ٱلَّذِينَ أَسَٰٓـُٔواْ بِمَا عَمِلُواْ وَيَجۡزِيَ ٱلَّذِينَ أَحۡسَنُواْ بِٱلۡحُسۡنَىٰ ۝ ﴾

"…That He may requite those, who do evil with that which they have done (i.e., punish them in Hell) and reward those who do good, with what is best (i.e., Paradise)." [Sūrah an-Najm (53):31]

Sūrah al-Fātihah establishes Faith in the Last Day and affirms this aspect of creed in the hearts of the believers through their numerous and constant repetition of this *Sūrah* in their days and nights. Allāh (جَلَّ وَعَلَا) says in this *Sūrah* about Himself:

﴿ مَٰلِكِ يَوۡمِ ٱلدِّينِ ۝ ﴾

"The Only Owner (and the Only Ruling Judge) of the Day of Recompense (i.e., the Day of Resurrection)." [Sūrah al-Fātihah (1):3]

Meaning: The Owner of the Day of Recompense and Punishment. It has been given this name because the people will be recompensed for their deeds and requited for what they have put forth in this life.

Allāh (جَلَّوَعَلَا) is ad-Dayyān (The Judge who requites, The King who is obeyed) as has come in the *Hadīth* of 'Abdullāh Ibn Unays (رضي الله عنه) who said: "I heard the Messenger of Allāh (صَلَّىاللهعَلَيْهِوَسَلَّمَ) saying:

يُحْشَرُ النَّاسُ يَوْمَ الْقِيَامَةِ حُفَاةً عُرَاةً غُرْلاً بُهْماً، قَالَ: قُلْنَا: وَمَا بُهْماً؟ قَالَ: لَيْسَ مَعَهُمْ شَيْءٌ، ثُمَّ يُنَادِيهِمْ بِصَوْتٍ يَسْمَعُهُ مِنْ قرب: أَنَا الْمَلِكُ أَنَا الدَّيَّانُ، وَلَا يَنْبَغِي لِأَحَدٍ مِنْ أَهْلِ النَّارِ أَنْ يَدْخُلَ النَّارَ، وَلَهُ عِنْدَ أَحَدٍ مِنْ أَهْلِ الْـجَنَّةِ حَقٌّ حَتَّى أَقَصَّهُ مِنْهُ؛ وَلَا يَنْبَغِي لِأَحَدٍ مِنْ أَهْلِ الْـجَنَّةِ أَنْ يَدْخُلَ الْـجَنَّةَ، وَلِأَحَدٍ مِنْ أَهْلِ النَّارِ عِنْدَهُ حَقٌّ، حَتَّى أَقَصَّهُ مِنْهُ، حَتَّى اللَّطْمَةَ، قَالَ: قُلْنَا كَيْفَ وَإِنَّمَا نَأْتِي اللهَ عَزَّ وَجَلَّ عُرَاةً غُرْلاً بُهْماً؟! قَالَ: بِالْـحَسَنَاتِ وَالسَّيِّئَاتِ.

"Allāh will gather the servants (the narrator said: or 'the people') naked, uncircumcised and without anything on the Day of Judgment.' We asked, 'What is meant by "without anything"?' The Prophet said, 'They will have nothing with them.' (The Prophet went on,) 'They will be called by a voice that is heard from afar just as it is heard

from nearby saying, 'I am the King. I am ad-Dayyān. None of the people of Paradise will enter Paradise while any of the people of the Fire are seeking him for some injustice he did to him until I avenge him. And none of the people of the Fire will enter the Fire while any of the people of Paradise are seeking him for an injustice he did to him until I avenge him even if it is just a slap.' We asked, 'How is this and we come to Allāh naked, uncircumcised and without anything?' He said, 'This applies to good actions and evil actions.'" [55]

Thus, this *Sūrah* establishes this great foundation in His (تَبَارَكَوَتَعَالَى) statement:

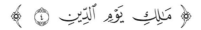

"The Only Owner (and the Only Ruling Judge) of the Day of Recompense (i.e., the Day of Resurrection)." [Sūrah al-Fātihah (1):3]

It similarly contains this meaning in other places, such as: **"All praise and thanks are for Allāh…"** Indeed, from the completeness of praising Allāh (جَلَّوَعَلَا)—for which reason this *Sūrah* was revealed—is His resurrecting the servants and recompensing them and rewarding the obedient from amongst them with the greatest and most virtuous of rewards; thus, when Allāh favors the people of

---

[55] Reported by Ahmad (3/495) and graded *Hasan Li Ghayrih* by al-Albānī (رَحِمَهُأَللَّه) in *Sahīh at-Targhīb* (3608)

Paradise on the Day of Resurrection with entering Paradise, they commence their entrance into it with the praise and exaltation of Allāh, saying:

﴿ ٱلْحَمْدُ لِلَّهِ ٱلَّذِى هَدَىٰنَا لِهَٰذَا وَمَا كُنَّا لِنَهْتَدِىَ لَوْلَآ أَنْ هَدَىٰنَا ٱللَّهُ ﴾

"All the praises and thanks be to Allāh, Who has guided us to this, and never could we have found guidance, were it not that Allāh had guided us!" [Sūrah al-A'rāf (7):43]

Allāh conferred upon them in their worldly-life with being obedient to him and with guidance and Faith; and will confer upon them on the Day of Judgment with entrance into His Paradise and attainment of His pleasure and rewards that He (جَلَّ وَعَلَا) has prepared for the people of Faith and his God-fearing servants. So, when they enter it, they will say:

﴿ ٱلْحَمْدُ لِلَّهِ ٱلَّذِى هَدَىٰنَا لِهَٰذَا ﴾

"All the praises and thanks be to Allāh, Who has guided us to this."

Meaning: If it was not for Him guiding us (تَبَارَكَ وَتَعَالَى), these blessings would not have occurred, and we would not have acquired these favors, virtues and this generosity and honor; these are completely from the grace and favor of Allāh (جَلَّ وَعَلَا), and indeed, He is the Bestower of Favor upon whomever He wishes from His servants.

His statement, **"The Lord of everything that exists,"** also affirms this tremendous foundation; because the Lord of everything that exists (جَلَّ وَعَلَا), is the One Who disposes of affairs and directs matters in this universe. And from the things that He directs in this universe (سبحانه) is His preparation of great rewards and splendid abodes for those that obey Him, and His severe punishment for those that disobey Him. Thus, he followed this verse up with His statement:

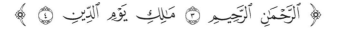

"The Most Gracious, the Most Merciful. The Only Owner (and the Only Ruling Judge) of the Day of Recompense (i.e., the Day of Resurrection)." [Sūrah al-Fātihah (1):2-3]

Therefore, the one who obeys Allāh (جَلَّ وَعَلَا) will earn the mercy and rewards of Allāh, and the one who disobeys Him will earn the displeasure and punishment of Allāh. The people are one of these two types, the obedient and the disobedient, a group in Paradise and a group in Hell.

Also, from the evidence of this *Sūrah* for this foundation is His statement (تَبَارَكَ وَتَعَالَى) regarding the state of the people of Faith:

﴿ إِيَّاكَ نَعْبُدُ وَإِيَّاكَ نَسْتَعِينُ ۝ ﴾

"You (Alone) we worship, and You (Alone) we ask for help (for each and everything)." [Sūrah al-Fātihah (1):4]

Indeed, whoever reflects over this magnificent verse and Allāh's extravagant wisdom in it, will realize that Allāh (سُبْحَانَهُ وَتَعَالَى) will never equate the *Muwahhid* (one who actualizes the Islamic monotheism of Allāh) servant with those who either deny or turn away from being obedient to the Lord of the universe. Thus, when Allāh (تَبَارَكَ وَتَعَالَى) mentioned Hell in the Noble *Qur'ān*, He said:

"None shall enter it save the most wretched, who denies and turns away." [Sūrah al-Layl (92):15-16]

Meaning: He denied the knowledge and turned away from the matter; so, he does not believe in the content that the Messengers have come with and nor does he abide by the commandments that they have come with. So, such a person will not be equated with the people of Faith and obedience, the people who seek assistance from Allāh (تَبَارَكَ وَتَعَالَى).

The three groups concerning the state of the people mentioned at the end of the *Sūrah*, similarly [works to establish the foundation of Faith in the Last Day]:

$$﴿ ٱهْدِنَا ٱلصِّرَٰطَ ٱلْمُسْتَقِيمَ ۝ صِرَٰطَ ٱلَّذِينَ أَنْعَمْتَ عَلَيْهِمْ غَيْرِ ٱلْمَغْضُوبِ عَلَيْهِمْ وَلَا ٱلضَّآلِّينَ ۝ ﴾$$

"Guide us to the Straight Way. The Way of those on whom You have bestowed Your Grace, not (the way) of those who earned Your Anger (such as the Jews), nor of those who went astray (such as the Christians)." [Sūrah al-Fātihah (1):5-7]

Allāh (جَلَّوَعَلَا) mentions that people are divided into three groups: a group bestowed with favor and they are the people of Faith and those upon Allāh's Straight Path which leads its people to the attainment of the pleasure of Allāh (تَبَارَكَوَتَعَالَى) and entrance into the gardens of bliss; a group who earned the wrath of Allāh (تَبَارَكَوَتَعَالَى); and a group who are lost and misguided from the Straight Path and the correct way.

Now, will all these groups be brought together in one abode on the Day of Judgment, in one place? Will they be considered equal? Certainly not, by Allāh! Rather, for those who have been favored will be Allāh's Paradise, blessings and rewards; and for those who earned His anger and went astray will be a blazing Fire that only the most wretched enter. So, there is a difference between the two groups: a group will be in Paradise and a group in the Fire.

Accordingly, if the believer contemplates over this wonderful *Sūrah*, he will continuously be mindful of *Īmān* in the Last Day. The day when he will be in front of Allāh (تَبَارَكَوَتَعَالَى). The believer becomes conscious that he will be rewarded, and Allāh (تَبَارَكَوَتَعَالَى) will be pleased with him if he fulfills the acts of obedience and his worship. If he leaves Allāh's Straight Path and strays from the correct way, he will earn the punishment of Allāh (تَبَارَكَوَتَعَالَى). And this is not a matter of mere wishes:

﴿ لَّيْسَ بِأَمَانِيِّكُمْ وَلَآ أَمَانِيِّ أَهْلِ ٱلْكِتَٰبِ مَن يَعْمَلْ سُوٓءًا يُجْزَ بِهِۦ ﴾

"It will not be following your desires (Muslims), nor those of the people of the Scripture (Jews and Christians), whosoever works evil, will have the recompense thereof." [Sūrah an-Nisā (4):123]

And Allāh (تَبَارَكَوَتَعَالَى) is Just:

"…And your Lord treats no one with injustice." [Sūrah al-Kahf (18):49]

This great day has many names that have been mentioned in the Noble *Qur'ān*, and the variety of its names is indicative of its different attributes. The following names have been mentioned in the *Qur'ān*:

- ❖ *Yawm at-Taghābun* (The Day of Reckoning),
- ❖ *as-Sākh-khah* (The Day of Resurrection's second blowing of the Trumpet),
- ❖ *al-Qāri'ah* (The Striking Hour),
- ❖ *at-Tāmmah* (The Catastrophe, i.e., the Day of Recompense),
- ❖ *al-Ghāshiyah* (The Overwhelming),
- ❖ *al-Yawm al-Ākhir* (The Last Day),
- ❖ *as-Sā'ah* (The Hour).

These are many names for this Day, and each name is indicative of one of its attributes. And from these names also is the one found in *Sūrah al-Fātihah*, the Day of Recompense, meaning, the Day of Compensation and Reckoning. It is a must that a believer has unwavering Faith in the Day of Judgement without any doubts and uncertainty. Whoever has doubt concerning the Day of Recompense has disbelieved, Allāh (سُبْحَانَهُوَتَعَالَى) said:

$$﴿ إِنَّمَا ٱلْمُؤْمِنُونَ ٱلَّذِينَ ءَامَنُواْ بِٱللَّهِ وَرَسُولِهِۦ ثُمَّ لَمْ يَرْتَابُواْ ﴾$$

"Only those are the believers who have believed in Allāh and His Messenger and afterward doubt not." [Sūrah al-Hujurāt (49):15]

Meaning: They have certainty with no doubts. It is an obligation to have firm faith, belief, trust, and conviction that there is a day of recompense and reckoning and standing in front of Allāh (تَبَارَكَوَتَعَالَى). As the believer lives his life, with every step that he takes, he is getting closer to the Last Day and further away from this world, as it was said:

$$إِنَّا لَنَفْرَحُ بِٱلْأَيَّام نَقْطَعُهَا \quad *** \quad وَكُلُّ يَوْمٍ مَضَى يُدْنِي مِنَ الْأَجَلِ$$

"We rejoice with every day that passes, yet, every passing day gets us closer to the appointed term." Meaning, the time of meeting Allāh and standing in before him.

'Alī Ibn Abī Tālib (رضي الله عنه) said:

اِرْتَحَلَتِ الدُّنْيَا مُدْبِرَةً وَارْتَحَلَتِ الْآخِرَةُ مُقْبِلَةً، وَلِكُلِّ وَاحِدَةٍ مِنْهُمَا بُنُونٌ، فَكُونُوا مِنْ أَبْنَاءِ الْآخِرَةِ وَلَا تَكُونُوا مِنْ أَبْنَاءِ الدُّنْيَا؛ فَإِنَّ الْيَوْمَ عَمَلٌ وَلَا حِسَابَ، وَغَداً حِسَابٌ وَلَا عَمَل.

"This world has departed with its back turned, and the Hereafter has advanced facing forward; each one has children, so be from the children of the Hereafter and not from those of this world; for indeed, today is a time for deeds and no accountability and tomorrow is a time for accountability and no deeds."[56]

Notice his words, "Tomorrow is a time for accountability and no deeds," because tomorrow—the Day of Recompense, the Day of Reckoning—is not a place to perform good deeds. Rather the place and time for deeds and actions occur are in this life. Ponder over the length of your existence in this life now compare it to the Day of Resurrection. The Prophet (عَلَيْهِ الصَّلَاةُ وَالسَّلَامُ) said:

أَعْمَارُ أُمَّتِي مَا بَيْنَ السِّتِّينَ إِلَى السَّبْعِينَ

---

[56] Added as commentary by al-Bukhārī—in a way indicative of its soundness—before *Hadīth* # 6418.

"The ages of (the people in) my nation will be between sixty and seventy."[57]

And many of the people might not reach sixty, their lives might come to an end in their youth, and from them are those that exceed sixty or seventy. However, generally speaking, the ages of the people are between sixty and seventy. This is the length of time spent in this worldly-life. Fifteen of those years are used before reaching puberty and religious obligations. Another third is spent in sleep—where nothing is counted against him. So, only thirty or thirty-years only remain.

However, on the fields of the Day of Resurrection before the reckoning starts—where the sun will only be a mile away from the creation, and the people sweat different amounts of sweat—the people will stand in this day for fifty thousand years!! So what comparison is there between the length of a person's life on this earth and fifty thousand years that he will have to stand on a plain that has no buildings, trees, plants, or anything else? And the people will equally stand on this day: the ruler and those that were ruled, the child and the adult, the man and the woman. They will stand barefooted, naked, uncircumcised, and mute. Then after this, the Lord (سُبْحَانَهُۥوَتَعَالَىٰ) will come to judge between the servants; because once the duration of their standing becomes too long, they will go to the prophets and ask them to intercede with Allāh to start the

---

[57] Reported by at-Tirmidhī (3550) and graded *Hasan* by al-Albānī (رَحِمَهُٱللَّه) in *Sahīh Sunan at-Tirmidhī* (3/460)

reckoning. They will come to Adam, but he will excuse himself. They will come to Nūh, but he will excuse himself. They will come to Ibrāhīm, but he will excuse himself. They will come to Mūsā, but he will excuse himself, then they will come to 'Īsā, but he will excuse himself; every single one of them will refer them to another [prophet]. And 'Īsā (عَلَيْهِ ٱلسَّلَامُ) will refer them to Muḥammad (صَلَّى ٱللَّهُ عَلَيْهِ وَسَلَّمَ), and he (عَلَيْهِ ٱلصَّلَاةُ وَٱلسَّلَامُ) will go and fall down in prostration to Allāh under the Throne. He will praise and exalt Allāh with praises and glorification that Allāh will teach him. Then it will be said:

يَا مُـحَمَّدَا! اِرْفَعْ رَأْسَكَ، سَلْ تُعْطَهُ، وَاشْفَعْ تَشْفَعُ

"O Muḥammad, raise your head; ask, and it would be granted; intercede, and intercession would be accepted."[58]

This is the 'station of praise and glory' that Allāh has mentioned:

﴿ عَسَىٰٓ أَن يَبْعَثَكَ رَبُّكَ مَقَامًا مَّحْمُودًا ۝ ﴾

"It may be that your Lord will raise you to Maqām Mahmūd (a station of praise and glory, i.e., the honor of intercession on the Day of Resurrection)." [Sūrah al-Isrā (17):79]

The early and later generations, as well as the prophets and messengers, will envy him for this (i.e., the permissible envy). So,

---

[58] Reported by al-Bukhārī (4712) and Muslim (194)

he (the Prophet) will intercede on behalf of the people with Allāh to start their Reckoning; and this is when the Lord will come, as Allāh (سُبْحَانَهُ وَتَعَالَى) mentions in the *Qur'ān*[59]:

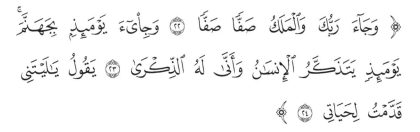

"And your Lord comes with the angels in rows, And Hell will be brought near that Day. On that Day will man remember, but how will that remembrance (then) avail him? He will say: "Alas! Would that I had sent forth (good deeds) for my life!" [Sūrah al-Fajr (89):22-24]

Man will then realize that the true life is the one in the Hereafter, as, for this life, it is one that will end. And regarding His statement:

﴿ وَجَآءَ رَبُّكَ وَٱلْمَلَكُ صَفًّا صَفًّا ۝ ﴾

"And your Lord comes with the angels in rows." [Sūrah al-Fajr (89):22]

---

[59] Reported by Ahmad (6/441) and authenticated by al-Albānī (رَحِمَهُ ٱللَّه) in *Sahīh al-Jāmi'* (1551)

It means that the angels will be lined up in rows behind other rows, surrounding the creation; then, the Lord (جَلَّوَعَلَا) will come to commence the judgment, and this is from the perfection of His Justice (سُبْحَانَهُوَتَعَالَى).

﴿ وَجِاْىَءَ يَوْمَئِذٍ بِجَهَـنَّمَ ﴾

"And Hell will be brought near that Day." [Sūrah al-Fajr (89): 23]

Hell will be dragged to the field of the gathering, as the Messenger of Allāh (صَلَّاللَّهُعَلَيْهِوَسَلَّمَ) said:

يُؤْتَى بِجَهَنَّمَ يَوْمَئِذٍ، لَهَا سَبْعُونَ أَلْفَ زِمَامٍ، مَعَ كُلِّ زِمَامٍ سَبْعُونَ أَلْف ملك يَـجُرُّونَهَا.

"Hell will be brought on that Day (the Day of Resurrection) with seventy thousand bridles, and with every bridle will be seventy thousand angels, pulling it."[60]

It will come angry and roaring at its people. We ask Allāh (جَلَّوَعَلَا) to grant us and you all refuge from the Fire (of Hell). Then a bridge will be erected over the brink of the Fire. It has been reported in

---

[60] Reported by Muslim (2842)

some *Ahādīth* that this bridge is thinner than a strand of hair[61] , and the people will be ordered to cross it; the speed with which they cross it will be according to their good deeds. The Prophet (صَلَّى ٱللَّهُ عَلَيْهِ وَسَلَّمَ) said:

الْمُؤْمِنُ عَلَيْهَا كَالطَّوْفِ وَكَالْبَرْقِ وَكَالرِّيحِ وَكَأَجَاوِيدَ الْـخَيْلِ وَالرِّكَابِ،

فَنَاجٍ مُسَلَّمٌ وَنَاجٍ مَـخْدُوشٌ وَمَكْدُوسٌ فِي نَارِ جَهَـنَّمَ.

"Some of the believers will cross the bridge as quickly as the blink of an eye, some others as quick as lightning, a strong wind, fast horses or she-camels. So, some will be safe without any harm; some will be safe after receiving some scratches, and some will fall down into Hell (Fire)."[62]

As for the disbeliever, after he is brought, he will walk on his head until he enters Hell. The scholars say: This is because, in this world, he (the disbeliever) turned the religion and Faith upside down, so he will be recompensed accordingly based on his actions; as Allāh (جَلَّ وَعَلَا) said:

---

[61] Abū Sa'īd al-Khudrī (رضي الله عنه) said: "It has reached me that the bridge is thinner than a piece of hair and sharper than a sword." Reported by Muslim (183) and there is proof for this in the *Hadīth* of 'Āishah, which is *Marfū:* "Hell has a bridge thinner than hair and sharper than a sword." Reported by Ahmad (6/110)
[62] Reported by al-Bukhārī (7439) and Muslim (183)

﴿ وَنَحْشُرُهُمْ يَوْمَ ٱلْقِيَٰمَةِ عَلَىٰ وُجُوهِهِمْ عُمْيًا وَبُكْمًا وَصُمًّا ۖ مَّأْوَىٰهُمْ جَهَنَّمُ ۖ ﴾

"We shall gather them together on the Day of Resurrection on their faces, blind, dumb, and deaf." [Sūrah al-Isrā (17):97]

On the authority of Qatādah who was informed by Anas Ibn Mālik (ﷺ) that a man said:

يَا نَبِيَّ اللهِ، يُـحْشَرُ الْكَافِرُ عَلَى وَجْهِهِ يَوْمَ الْقِيَامَةِ؟! قَالَ: أَلَيْسَ الَّذِي أَمْشَاهُ عَلَى الرِّجْلَيْنِ فِي الدُّنْيَا، قَادِراً عَلَى أَنْ يُمْشِيهِ عَلَى وَجْهِهِ يَوْمَ الْقِيَامَةِ؟، قَالَ قَتَادَةُ: بَلَى وَعِزَّةِ رَبِّنَا.

"O Prophet of Allāh, how will the non-believers be assembled on the Day of Resurrection (by crawling) on their faces? Thereupon he said: 'Is He Who can make them walk on their feet in this world not able to make them walk upon their faces on the Day of Resurrection?' Qatādah said: Of course, it is so, by the Might of our Lord."[63]

Then, with regards to the people entering Hell or being saved from it and entering Paradise, they will be divided into three groups:

---

[63] Reported by al-Bukhārī (4860) and Muslim (2806)

The first group: A group that will enter Hell and abide therein for eternity; they will not be killed, so they will not die and nor will the severity of the torment be lightened for them. And this is a punishment for every disbeliever, polytheist, and atheist; as Allāh (تَبَارَكَ وَتَعَالَى) said:

وَٱلَّذِينَ كَفَرُواْ لَهُمْ نَارُ جَهَنَّمَ لَا يُقْضَىٰ عَلَيْهِمْ فَيَمُوتُواْ وَلَا يُخَفَّفُ عَنْهُم مِّنْ عَذَابِهَا كَذَٰلِكَ نَجْزِي كُلَّ كَفُورٍ ۝ وَهُمْ يَصْطَرِخُونَ فِيهَا رَبَّنَا أَخْرِجْنَا نَعْمَلْ صَٰلِحًا غَيْرَ ٱلَّذِي كُنَّا نَعْمَلُ أَوَلَمْ نُعَمِّرْكُم مَّا يَتَذَكَّرُ فِيهِ مَن تَذَكَّرَ وَجَآءَكُمُ ٱلنَّذِيرُ فَذُوقُواْ فَمَا لِلظَّٰلِمِينَ مِن نَّصِيرٍ ۝

"But those who disbelieve (in the Oneness of Allāh - Islāmic Monotheism) for them will be the Fire of Hell. Neither will it have a complete killing effect on them so that they die, nor shall its torment be lightened for them. Thus, do We requite every disbeliever! Therein they will cry: "Our Lord! Bring us out, we shall do righteous good deeds, not (the evil deeds) that we used to do." (Allāh will reply): "Did We not give you lives long enough, so that whosoever would receive admonition, could receive it? And the warner came to you. So, taste you (the evil of your deeds). For the Zālimūn (polytheists and wrong-doers), there is no helper." [Sūrah Fātir (35):37]

The second group: A group that will enter Paradise right away without reckoning or punishment; and they are those who 'followed a middle course' and those who were 'foremost in good deeds.' Allāh (سُبْحَانَهُوَتَعَالَى) said:

$$﴿ ثُمَّ أَوْرَثْنَا ٱلْكِتَٰبَ ٱلَّذِينَ ٱصْطَفَيْنَا مِنْ عِبَادِنَا فَمِنْهُمْ ظَالِمٌ لِّنَفْسِهِۦ وَمِنْهُم مُّقْتَصِدٌ وَمِنْهُمْ سَابِقٌۢ بِٱلْخَيْرَٰتِ بِإِذْنِ ٱللَّهِ ذَٰلِكَ هُوَ ٱلْفَضْلُ ٱلْكَبِيرُ ۝ جَنَّٰتُ عَدْنٍ يَدْخُلُونَهَا ﴾$$

"Then We gave the (Book the *Qur'ān*) as inheritance to such of Our slaves whom We chose (the followers of Muḥammad صَلَّىٱللَّهُعَلَيْهِوَسَلَّمَ). Then of them are some who wrong their own selves, and of them are some who follow a middle course, and of them are some who are, by Allāh's Leave, foremost in good deeds. That (inheritance of the *Qur'ān*) is indeed a great grace. 'Adn (Eden) Paradise (everlasting Gardens) will they enter." [Sūrah Fāṭir (35): 32-33]

So as for the three types of people mentioned here—those who wrong themselves, those who follow a middle course and those who are foremost in good deeds—the ones who followed a middle course and the ones who were foremost in good deeds will enter the Gardens of Eden (Paradise) without reckoning and punishment. The 'one who follows a middle course' is he who fulfills the commandments and abstains from the prohibitions; the 'one who is foremost in good deeds' is he who exceeds this by performing the strongly recommended deeds and abstains from the disliked matters and competes in performing the good deeds.

The third group: of the three is the 'one who wronged himself.' This group will be subject to punishment and reckoning. If Allāh (تَبَارَكَ وَتَعَالَى) punishes them in the Fire of Hell on the Day of Resurrection, He (جَلَّ وَعَلَا) will not make them abide in it for eternity. Only the disbeliever and polytheist will permanently abide in Hell. As for those who committed major sins, if they enter the Fire on the Day of Resurrection because of their bad deeds and major sins that are less than the sin of disbelief in Allāh (تَبَارَكَ وَتَعَالَى), they will remain therein only to be purified and cleansed. Then they will be deserving of entering Paradise. And Paradise is an abode of absolute purity (i.e., complete goodness) for the pure ones. For this reason, the angels will say:

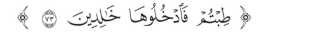

"You have done well, so enter here to abide therein."
[Sūrah az-Zumar (39):73]

If a person has goodness in him, but with some filth, surely, he will be cleansed of this filth; then, he will enter Paradise after the purification and cleansing. So, the people of *Tawhīd* who will enter the Fire, is one of cleansing and purification. In contrast, the disbelievers' entering it is one of eternal torment. These are the three groups that the people will be divided into on the Day of Resurrection.

Once the disobedient from the people of *Tawḥīd* have completely exited Hell and entered into Paradise, death will be slaughtered, and it will be said:

"O people of Paradise, an eternity for you and no death. O people of Hell, an eternity for you and no death."

On the authority of Abī Sa'īd al-Khudrī (رضي الله عنه) who said:

يُؤْتَى بِالْمَوْتِ كَهَيْئَةِ كَبْشٍ أَمْلَحَ فَيُنَادِي مُنَادٍ يَا أَهْلَ الْجَنَّةِ، فَيَشْرَئِبُّونَ وَيَنْظُرُونَ فَيَقُولُ هَلْ تَعْرِفُونَ هَذَا فَيَقُولُونَ نَعَمْ هَذَا الْمَوْتُ، وَكُلُّهُمْ قَدْ رَآهُ، ثُمَّ يُنَادِي يَا أَهْلَ النَّارِ، فَيَشْرَئِبُّونَ وَيَنْظُرُونَ، فَيَقُولُ هَلْ تَعْرِفُونَ هَذَا فَيَقُولُونَ نَعَمْ هَذَا الْمَوْتُ، وَكُلُّهُمْ قَدْ رَآهُ، فَيُذْبَحُ ثُمَّ يَقُولُ يَا أَهْلَ الْجَنَّةِ، خُلُودٌ فَلاَ مَوْتَ، وَيَا أَهْلَ النَّارِ، خُلُودٌ فَلاَ مَوْتَ ثُمَّ قَرَأَ (وَأَنْذِرْهُمْ يَوْمَ الْحَسْرَةِ إِذْ قُضِيَ الأَمْرُ وَهُمْ فِي غَفْلَةٍ) وَهَؤُلاَءِ فِي غَفْلَةٍ أَهْلُ الدُّنْيَا (وَهُمْ لاَ يُؤْمِنُونَ)

"The Messenger of Allāh (صلى الله عليه وسلم) said: 'On the Day of Resurrection Death will be brought forward in the shape of a black and white ram. Then a call maker will call, 'O people of Paradise!' Thereupon they will stretch their necks and look carefully. The caller will say, 'Do you know this?' They will say, 'Yes, this is Death.' By then all of them will have seen it. Then it will be announced again, 'O

people of Hell!' They will stretch their necks and look carefully. The caller will say, 'Do you know this?' They will say, 'Yes, this is Death.' And by then all of them will have seen it. Then it (the ram) will be slaughtered and the caller will say, 'O people of Paradise! Eternity for you and no death, O people of Hell! Eternity for you and no death.' Then the Prophet, recited: 'And warn them of the Day of grief and distress when the case has been decided, while (now) they are in a state of carelessness.' 'These people that are in a state of carelessness are the people of this world: '...and they do not believe.'" [Sūrah Maryam (19): 39][64]

The Book (the *Qur'ān*) and the Sunnah have come with a clear explanation and a sufficient clarification regarding what will take place on that great Day from the recompense, the reckoning, the punishments and the division of the people into two groups: A group in Paradise and a group in Hell. So, from the great foundations and principles of Faith is *Īmān* in the Last Day. And whoever does not believe in the Last day is a disbeliever in Allāh; Allāh (تَبَارَكَوَتَعَالَى) will not accept anything from them. For this reason, there are numerous texts that mention this (belief in the Last Day) along with the other articles of *Īmān*, like the statement of Allāh (تَبَارَكَوَتَعَالَى):

---

[64] Reported by al-Bukhārī (4830) and Muslim (2849)

﴿ ۞ لَّيۡسَ ٱلۡبِرَّ أَن تُوَلُّواْ وُجُوهَكُمۡ قِبَلَ ٱلۡمَشۡرِقِ وَٱلۡمَغۡرِبِ وَلَٰكِنَّ ٱلۡبِرَّ مَنۡ ءَامَنَ بِٱللَّهِ وَٱلۡيَوۡمِ ٱلۡأَخِرِ وَٱلۡمَلَٰٓئِكَةِ وَٱلۡكِتَٰبِ وَٱلنَّبِيِّـۧنَ ﴾

"It is not al-Birr (piety, righteousness, and each and every act of obedience to Allāh, etc.) that you turn your faces towards east and (or) west (in prayers); but al-Birr is (the quality of) the one who believes in Allāh, the Last Day, the Angels, the Book, the Prophets." [Sūrah al-Baqarah (2): 177]

And Allāh (تَبَارَكَ وَتَعَالَى) said:

﴿ ءَامَنَ ٱلرَّسُولُ بِمَآ أُنزِلَ إِلَيۡهِ مِن رَّبِّهِۦ وَٱلۡمُؤۡمِنُونَۚ كُلٌّ ءَامَنَ بِٱللَّهِ وَمَلَٰٓئِكَتِهِۦ وَكُتُبِهِۦ وَرُسُلِهِۦ لَا نُفَرِّقُ بَيۡنَ أَحَدٍ مِّن رُّسُلِهِۦۚ وَقَالُواْ سَمِعۡنَا وَأَطَعۡنَاۖ غُفۡرَانَكَ رَبَّنَا وَإِلَيۡكَ ٱلۡمَصِيرُ ۝ ﴾

"The Messenger (Muḥammad ﷺ) believes in what has been sent down to him from his Lord, and (so do) the believers. Each one believes in Allāh, His Angels, His Books, and His Messengers. (They say), "We make no distinction between one another of His Messengers" and

they say, "We hear, and we obey. (We seek) Your Forgiveness, our Lord, and to You is the return (of all)." [Sūrah al-Baqarah (2):285]

Allāh mentioned these principles: Belief in Allāh, belief in the Angels, belief in the Book (the *Qur'ān*), belief in the Messengers and belief in the Last Day. And Allāh (تَبَارَكَ وَتَعَالَى) said:

$$﴿ يَٰٓأَيُّهَا ٱلَّذِينَ ءَامَنُوٓاْ ءَامِنُواْ بِٱللَّهِ وَرَسُولِهِۦ وَٱلۡكِتَٰبِ ٱلَّذِى$$

$$نَزَّلَ عَلَىٰ رَسُولِهِۦ وَٱلۡكِتَٰبِ ٱلَّذِىٓ أَنزَلَ مِن قَبۡلُ وَمَن يَكۡفُرۡ$$

$$بِٱللَّهِ وَمَلَٰٓئِكَتِهِۦ وَكُتُبِهِۦ وَرُسُلِهِۦ وَٱلۡيَوۡمِ ٱلۡأٓخِرِ فَقَدۡ ضَلَّ ضَلَٰلَۢا$$

$$بَعِيدًا ﴿١٣٦﴾ ﴾$$

"O you who believe! Believe in Allāh, and His Messenger (Muḥammad صَلَّى ٱللَّهُ عَلَيْهِ وَسَلَّمَ), and the Book (the *Qur'ān*) which He has sent down to His Messenger, and the Scripture which He sent down to those before (him), and whosoever disbelieves in Allāh, His Angels, His Books, His Messengers, and the Last Day, then indeed he has strayed far away." [Sūrah an-Nisā (4):136]

Belief in Allāh and in the Last Day are principles from the principles of *Īmān* which are the pillars of the religion upon which it stands. Thus, when Jibrīl came—in the famous *Hadīth*—to the Prophet (صَلَّى ٱللَّهُ عَلَيْهِ وَسَلَّمَ) and he asked him about *Īmān*. The Prophet said:

أَنْ تُؤْمِنَ بِاللهِ وَمَلَائِكَتِهِ وَكُتُبِهِ وَرُسُلِهِ وَالْيَوْمِ الْآخِرِ، وَتُؤْمِنَ بِالْقَدَرِ خَيْرِهِ وَشَرِّهِ.

"It is that you believe in Allāh, His angels, His books, His messengers and the Last Day and that you believe in preordainment, its bad and good."[65]

And as the believer recites the Book of Allāh (جَلَّ وَعَلَا), he increases in *Īmān* because the clear verses and manifest proofs for this Day and the standing in front of Allāh and returning to Him are many in the Book of Allāh and the Sunnah of His Prophet (صَلَّى اللَّهُ عَلَيْهِ وَسَلَّمَ). You will come across many of these verses in the *Qur'ān*:

﴿ إِنَّ إِلَىٰ رَبِّكَ ٱلرُّجْعَىٰ ۞ ﴾

"Surely! unto your Lord is the return." [Sūrah al-'Alaq (96): 8]

﴿ وَإِلَيْكَ ٱلْمَصِيرُ ۞ ﴾

"And to You is the return (of all)." [Sūrah al-Baqarah (2):285]

﴿ إِنَّ إِلَيْنَآ إِيَابَهُمْ ۞ ثُمَّ إِنَّ عَلَيْنَا حِسَابَهُم ۞ ﴾

---

[65] Reported by Muslim (8)

Verily, to Us will be their return; (25) Then, for Us will be their reckoning." [Sūrah al-Ghāshiyah (88):25-26]

These verses and other than them guide you and clarify to you that your end and return is to Allāh; and that you will stand in front of Him and that He (تَبَارَكَوَتَعَالَى) will hold you to account. So, the believer continues to increase in his conviction and *Īmān* in the Last Day through reading the *Qur'ān*.

The scholars say that *Īmān* in the Last Day is two levels:

The First Level: This is what is required of every Muslim, and if it is not present in a person, then he is a disbeliever and not from the people of this religion. And it is that a person considers as truth, believes and holds that there will be a day for reckoning, for punishment, for standing before Allāh (سُبْحَانَهُوَتَعَالَى), in which Allāh (عَزَّوَجَلَّ) will recompense the people for their deeds and what they put forth from actions in this life. This is called '*al-Īmān al-Jāzim*' (the unwavering belief); the meaning of 'unwavering' is that it is not mixed with doubt or suspicion and we have already mentioned the statement of Allāh (تَبَارَكَوَتَعَالَى):

﴾ إِنَّمَا ٱلْمُؤْمِنُونَ ٱلَّذِينَ ءَامَنُوا۟ بِٱللَّهِ وَرَسُولِهِۦ ثُمَّ لَمْ يَرْتَابُوا۟ ﴿

"Only those are the believers who have believed in Allāh and His Messenger and afterward doubt not." [Sūrah al-Hujurāt (49):15]

It is *Īmān* that has no suspicion or doubt. If there is doubt found in one's belief in the Last day or in any of the principles of Faith, then His *Īmān* will be negated—it will not remain with the existence of doubt.

The Second Level: This is '*al-Īmān ar-Rāsikh*' (the well-established belief) in the Last Day. And this is higher than '*al-Īmān al-Jāzim*' (the unwavering belief). 'Well-established belief' means that a servant brings this Day to mind and constantly fears it, as well as being conscious of the meeting with Allāh (تَبَارَكَ وَتَعَالَى) and standing before Him—his mind is forever occupied with preparing for this Day. Thus, the people with this level of *Īmān* will obtain a high status and a lofty station when they meet Allāh (تَبَارَكَ وَتَعَالَى):

$$﴿ أَهْلِنَا مُشْفِقِينَ ۝ فَمَنَّ ٱللَّهُ عَلَيْنَا وَوَقَىٰنَا عَذَابَ ٱلسَّمُومِ ۝ ﴾$$

"Saying: "Aforetime, we were afraid (of the punishment of Allāh) among our families. "So Allāh has been gracious to us and has saved us from the torment of the Fire." [Sūrah at-Tūr (52):27]

$$﴿ فَأَمَّا مَنْ أُوتِيَ كِتَٰبَهُۥ بِيَمِينِهِۦ فَيَقُولُ هَآؤُمُ ٱقْرَءُوا۟ كِتَٰبِيَهْ ۝ إِنِّى ظَنَنتُ أَنِّى مُلَٰقٍ حِسَابِيَهْ ۝ ﴾$$

Then as for him who will be given his Record in his right hand will say: "Here! Read my Record! Surely, I did

believe that I shall meet my Account!" [Sūrah al-Hāqqah (69):19-20]

"I did believe," meaning that I firmly believed while in the worldly-life that I would meet my reckoning and judgment. And bringing this to mind is really important; it has excellent effects on a person's behavior. It has come in a *Hadīth* that the Messenger of Allāh (ﷺ) would place his right hand under his cheek when he would lie down and say:

اللَّهُمَّ قِنِي عَذَابَكَ يَوْمَ تَبْعَثُ عِبَادَكَ

"O Allāh, safeguard me from Your Punishment the Day You resurrect your slaves."[66]

He (ﷺ) would regularly remind himself of the reckoning, resurrection, and standing before Allāh. So, the 'well-established Faith' entails that a person is conscious of the return to Allāh (تَبَارَكَوَتَعَالَى), the departure from the worldly life, and the standing of the servants in front of Allāh (جَلَّوَعَلَا).

This high level of Faith which is known as '*al-Īmān ar-Rāsikh*' (the well-established belief) can only be achieved through reading the *Qur'ān* and *Ahādīth* (prophetic narrations) and pondering over the verses and texts which contain a clarification of this matter. And the people of knowledge have authored numerous writings concerning

---

[66] Reported by Abū Dāwūd (5045) and authenticated by al-Albānī (رَحِمَهُاللَّه) in *Sahīh Sunan Abī Dāwūd* (3/240)

Belief in the Last Day. Some of them have writings concerning the Fire, like the book, *an-Nār (The Fire)* or *al-Jannah (Paradise)* or *Ahwāl Yawm al-Qiyāmah (The Terrors of the Day of Judgment)*; or concerning some of the details of events that occur on the Day of Judgment like The Scale, the Bridge or what is similar to that. And the intent of the authors of these books was not to merely give evidence for '*al-Īmān al-Jāzim*' (the unwavering belief), rather so that the believer can read them and cause his *Īmān* to become well-established, stronger and more stable. So that he can be acquainted with the close details of what will take place on the Day—thus, his link with Allāh will strengthen and his desire for His Mercy, Virtue, and Grace will increase, as well as his fear and apprehension of the punishment, wrath, and displeasure of Allāh (تَبَارَكَ وَتَعَالَى). Therefore, the well-established *Īmān* can only be earned through such readings.

You will notice that in many texts of the *Qur'ān* and the Sunnah, Allāh (جَلَّ وَعَلَا) will mention a righteous act that He is pleased with or a prohibition that He is forbidding His servant from; and He will mention before it *Īmān* in Allāh and the Last Day, as is in His statement:

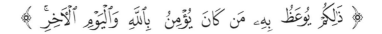

"That will be an admonition given to him who believes in Allāh and the Last Day." [Sūrah at-Ṭalāq (65):2]

And in His statement:

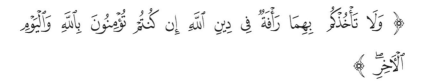

"Let not pity withhold you in their case, in a punishment prescribed by Allāh, if you believe in Allāh and the Last Day." [Sūrah an-Nūr (24):2]

Similarly, in the Sunnah, various *Aḥādīth* mention orders or prohibitions tied with *Īmān* in the Last Day, like his statement (عَلَيْهِٱلصَّلَاةُوَٱلسَّلَامُ):

مَنْ كَانَ يُؤْمِنُ بِاللَّهِ وَالْيَوْمِ الآخِرِ فَلاَ يُؤْذِ جَارَهُ، وَمَنْ كَانَ يُؤْمِنُ بِاللَّهِ وَالْيَوْمِ الآخِرِ فَلْيُكْرِمْ ضَيْفَهُ، وَمَنْ كَانَ يُؤْمِنُ بِاللَّهِ وَالْيَوْمِ الآخِرِ فَلْيَقُلْ خَيْرًا أَوْ لِيَصْمُتْ

"He who believes in Allāh and the Last Day let him not harm his neighbor; he who believes in Allāh and the Last Day let him show hospitality to his guest; he who believes in Allāh and the Last Day let him speak good or remain silent."[67]

---

[67] Reported by al-Bukhārī (6078) and Muslim (47)

لَا يَحِلُّ لِامْرَأَةٍ تُؤْمِنُ بِاللَّهِ وَالْيَوْمِ الآخِرِ أَنْ تُسَافِرَ مَسِيرَةَ يَوْمٍ وَلَيْلَةٍ لَيْسَ مَعَهَا حُرْمَةٌ

"It is not permissible for a woman who believes in Allāh and the Last Day to make a journey of one day and night unless she is accompanied by a *Mahram* (husband or any other relative to whom she is prohibited from marrying)."[68]

And the intent behind this is so that Belief in Allāh and the Last Day is brought to mind; as for reminding ourselves with our belief in Allāh, then this is because Allāh (جَلَّ وَعَلَا) is the One Whom we intend with our deeds. As for bringing belief in the Last Day to mind, then this is because this is the Day of Recompense for the deeds that we worked. Thus, it is a must to be mindful of and bring the following to mind, especially when a servant is getting ready to perform an act of worship or refrain from sin.

This belief continues to guide and direct the servant to every good, success, and happiness in this world and the next. Still, if he forgets about this Belief or pretends to forget about it, he will start to get weak, and his religion and *Īmān* will also start to weaken. Hence, our need to strengthen our hearts with Faith in Allāh, the Last Day, and the rest of the pillars of *Īmān* is truly dire:

---

[68] Reported by al-Bukhārī (1088) and Muslim (1339)

﴿ ۞ قَالَتِ ٱلْأَعْرَابُ ءَامَنَّا قُل لَّمْ تُؤْمِنُوا۟ وَلَٰكِن قُولُوٓا۟ أَسْلَمْنَا وَلَمَّا يَدْخُلِ ٱلْإِيمَٰنُ فِى قُلُوبِكُمْ ﴾

"The Bedouins say: "We believe." Say to them: "You believe not, instead say, 'We have surrendered (in Islām),' for Faith has not yet entered your hearts." [Sūrah al-Hujurāt (49):14]

Meaning: Faith has not firmly settled in your hearts. Because the people of Faith do not all have the same level of *Īmān*. The Companions (of the Prophet) (رَضِيَ ٱللَّهُ عَنْهُمْ) would sit with the Prophet (صَلَّى ٱللَّهُ عَلَيْهِ وَسَلَّمَ). He would admonish them and remind them about the Last Day, and it would be as if they saw, with their eyes, Paradise and Hell! And he (صَلَّى ٱللَّهُ عَلَيْهِ وَسَلَّمَ) said:

مَنْ سَرَّه أَنْ يَنْظُرَ إِلَى يَوْمِ الْقِيَامَةِ كَأَنَّهُ رَأَى عَيْنٍ، فَلْيَقْرَأْ: ﴿ إِذَا ٱلشَّمْسُ كُوِّرَتْ ۝ ﴾ ، وَ ﴿ إِذَا ٱلسَّمَآءُ ٱنفَطَرَتْ ۝ ﴾ ، وَ ﴿ إِذَا ٱلسَّمَآءُ ٱنشَقَّتْ ۝ ﴾

"Whoever wishes to look at the Day of Resurrection as if he sees it with his eye, then let him recite: *'Idhash-shamsu*

kuwwirat'(at-Takwīr) and *'Idhas-samā un-fatarat'* (al-Infitār) and *'Idhas-samā un-shaqqat'* (al-Inshiqāq)"[69]

And the meaning of this is that reading these chapters (mentioned in the *Hadīth*) while pondering over them will cause you to visualize the Day of Resurrection and its terrors as if you are looking at them.

The Last Day for each person will actually commence with the departure of his soul from his body; thus, the scholars say: "The one who died, his Resurrection has begun." This is because as soon as a person dies, their actions will cease—he will not be able to pray, fast, give charity or pay the mandatory alms. One of the *Salaf* once held his soul to account, saying: "O self, if you die, who will offer *Salāh* on your behalf? Who will perform Hajj for you? Who will fast for you? Who will do this and that for you…?"

And the grave is the first stage from the stages of the Hereafter, and in it, a person will either find bliss or torment; and it starts once the diseased is entered into his grave. This is why the scholars define Faith in the Last Day as Belief in everything that will take place after death, starting from the point where a person is entered into his grave. On the authority of Abū Hurairah (رضي الله عنه) who narrated that the Messenger of Allāh (صَلَّى اللَّهُ عَلَيْهِ وَسَلَّمَ) said:

إِذَا قُبِرَ الْمَيِّتُ - أَوْ قَالَ أَحَدُكُمْ أَتَاهُ مَلَكَانِ أَسْوَدَانِ أَزْرَقَانِ يُقَالُ لِأَحَدِهِمَا الْمُنْكَرُ وَالآخَرُ النَّكِيرُ فَيَقُولاَنِ مَا كُنْتَ تَقُولُ فِي هَذَا الرَّجُلِ

---

[69] Reported by at-Tirmidhī (3333) and authenticated by al-Albānī (رحمه الله) in *Sahīh Sunan at-Tirmidhī* (3/364)

فَيَقُولُ مَا كَانَ يَقُولُ هُوَ عَبْدُ اللَّهِ وَرَسُولُهُ أَشْهَدُ أَنْ لاَ إِلَهَ إِلاَّ اللَّهُ وَأَنَّ

مُحَمَّدًا عَبْدُهُ وَرَسُولُهُ . فَيَقُولاَنِ قَدْ كُنَّا نَعْلَمُ أَنَّكَ تَقُولُ هَذَا . ثُمَّ يُفْسَحُ

لَهُ فِي قَبْرِهِ سَبْعُونَ ذِرَاعًا فِي سَبْعِينَ ثُمَّ يُنَوَّرُ لَهُ فِيهِ ثُمَّ يُقَالُ لَهُ نَمْ . فَيَقُولُ

أَرْجِعُ إِلَى أَهْلِي فَأُخْبِرُهُمْ فَيَقُولاَنِ نَمْ كَنَوْمَةِ الْعَرُوسِ الَّذِي لاَ يُوقِظُهُ إِلاَّ

أَحَبُّ أَهْلِهِ إِلَيْهِ . حَتَّى يَبْعَثَهُ اللَّهُ مِنْ مَضْجَعِهِ ذَلِكَ . وَإِنْ كَانَ مُنَافِقًا

قَالَ سَمِعْتُ النَّاسَ يَقُولُونَ فَقُلْتُ مِثْلَهُ لاَ أَدْرِي . فَيَقُولاَنِ قَدْ كُنَّا نَعْلَمُ

أَنَّكَ تَقُولُ ذَلِكَ . فَيُقَالُ لِلأَرْضِ الْتَئِمِي عَلَيْهِ . فَتَلْتَئِمُ عَلَيْهِ . فَتَخْتَلِفُ

فِيهَا أَضْلاَعُهُ فَلاَ يَزَالُ فِيهَا مُعَذَّبًا حَتَّى يَبْعَثَهُ اللَّهُ مِنْ مَضْجَعِهِ ذَلِكَ

"When the deceased - or he said when one of you - is buried, two angels, black and blue (eyed) come to him. One of them is called al-Munkar and the other an-Nakīr. They say: 'What did you use to say about this man?' So, he says what he used to say (before death). 'He is Allāh's slave and His Messenger. I testify that none has the right to be worshipped, but Allāh and that Muḥammad is His slave and His Messenger.' So, they say: 'We knew that you would say this.' Then his grave is expanded to seventy by seventy cubits, and then it is illuminated for him. Then it is said to him: 'Sleep.' So, he says: 'Can I return to my family to inform them?' They say: 'Sleep as a newlywed, whom none awakens but the dearest of his family until Allāh resurrects him from his resting place.' If he was a hypocrite, he would say: 'I heard people saying something,

so I said the same; I do not know.' So, they said: 'We knew you would say that.' So, the earth is told: 'Constrict him.' So, it constricts around him, squeezing his ribs together. He continues being punished like that until Allāh resurrects him from his resting place."[70]

And these (questions that one is asked in the grave) are referred to as 'the three principles' by the people of knowledge because they are the first questions that a person is asked as soon as he enters his grave. It is a test that requires adequate preparation. So, what is our preparation for these 'three principles'? And indeed, the Prophet (عَلَيْهِ ٱلصَّلَاةُوَٱلسَّلَامُ) has said:

ذَاقَ طَعْمَ الْإِيمَانِ مَنْ رَضِيَ بِاللهِ رَبًّا، وَبِالْإِسْلَامِ دِيناً، وَبِمُحَمَّدٍ صَلَّى اللهُ عَلَيْهِ وَسَلَّمَ نَبِيًّا.

"He has found the taste of Faith (Īmān) who is content with Allāh as his Lord, with Islām as his religion (code of life) and with Muḥammad (صَلَّىٱللَّهُعَلَيْهِوَسَلَّمَ) as his Prophet."[71]

The believer is endowed with gifts in his grave while a disbeliever is punished in his, as Allāh (سُبْحَانَهُوَتَعَالَى) said:

---

[70] Reported by at-Tirmidhī (1071) and authenticated by al-Albānī (رَحِمَهُٱللَّهُ) in *Sahīh Sunan at-Tirmidhī* (1/544)
[71] Reported by Muslim (24)

$$\text{﴿ ٱلنَّارُ يُعْرَضُونَ عَلَيْهَا غُدُوًّا وَعَشِيًّا ۚ وَيَوْمَ تَقُومُ ٱلسَّاعَةُ}$$

$$\text{أَدْخِلُوا ءَالَ فِرْعَوْنَ أَشَدَّ ٱلْعَذَابِ ۝ ﴾}$$

"The Fire; they are exposed to it, morning and afternoon, and on the Day when the Hour will be established (it will be said to the angels): "Cause Fir'awn's (Pharaoh) people to enter the severest torment!" [Sūrah Ghāfir (40):46]

Pharaoh's people are exposed to the Fire every morning and afternoon until the Day of Resurrection. On this Day, they will enter the severest punishment. And the Prophet (عَلَيْهِ ٱلصَّلَاةُ وَٱلسَّلَامُ) said: "The punishment of the grave is real."[72] And he (عَلَيْهِ ٱلصَّلَاةُ وَٱلسَّلَامُ) said: "Seek refuge with Allāh from the punishment of the grave."[73] And he (عَلَيْهِ ٱلصَّلَاةُ وَٱلسَّلَامُ) said:

$$\text{إِذَا تَشَهَّدَ أَحَدُكُمْ فَلْيَسْتَعِذْ بِاللهِ مِنْ أَرْبَعٍ، يَقُولُ:}$$

"When anyone of you has done his Tashahhud during *Salāh* (prayer), let him seek refuge in Allāh against four things and say:

---

[72] Reported by Ahmad (4/174) and authenticated by al-Albānī (رَحِمَهُ ٱللَّهُ) in *as-Sahīhah* (1377)

[73] Reported by Muslim (2867)

اللَّهُمَّ إِنِّي أَعُوذُ بِكَ مِن عَذَابِ جَهَنَّم، ومِن عَذاب القَبْرِ ومِن فِتْنَة المَحْيا والمَمَات، ومِن شَرِّ فِتْنَة المَسِيح الدَّجَّال

'O Allāh! I seek refuge with You from the torment of Hell, the torment of the grave, from the trials of life and death, and from the trial of _al-Masīh ad-Dajjāl_ (Antichrist).'"[74]

And when will a person die and separate from this life? He does not know! It could be in an hour or two, or in a day or two. Allāh (سُبْحَانَهُوَتَعَالَى) says:

$$ ﴿ ۞ ۳۸ لِكُلِّ أَجَلٍ كِتَابٌ ۞ ﴾ $$

"For every matter, there is a Decree (from Allāh)." [Sūrah ar-Ra'ad (13):38]

And he (سُبْحَانَهُوَتَعَالَى) says:

$$ ﴿ ۞ فَإِذَا جَاءَ أَجَلُهُمْ لَا يَسْتَأْخِرُونَ سَاعَةً وَلَا يَسْتَقْدِمُونَ ۳٤ ﴾ $$

"When their term comes, neither can they delay it, nor can they advance it an hour (or a moment)." [Sūrah al-'Arāf (7):34]

Thus, it befits a person to be prepared and ready for this Day, keeping in mind that he will meet Allāh (تَبَارَكَوَتَعَالَى) and stand before

---

[74] Reported by Muslim (588)

Him and that He will recompense and hold the reckoning; and that the Scale on the Day of Resurrection will calculate deeds that are the weight of an atom:

$$﴿ فَمَن يَعۡمَلۡ مِثۡقَالَ ذَرَّةٍ خَيۡرًا يَرَهُ ۞ وَمَن يَعۡمَلۡ مِثۡقَالَ ذَرَّةٍ شَرًّا يَرَهُ ۞ ﴾$$

"So, whosoever does good equal to the weight of an atom (or a small ant) shall see it. And whosoever does evil equal to the weight of an atom (or a small ant), shall see it." (az-Zalzalah (99):7-8]

We ask Allāh for safety and security and success to fulfill what He loves and is pleased with.

7TH GUIDELINE: ESTABLISHMENT OF THE BELIEF IN *AL-QADAR* (DIVINE PRE-DECREE

From the guidelines of this *Sūrah* is its clarification and affirmation of *Īmān* in the Pre-Decree of Allāh (سُبْحَانَهُوَتَعَالَ) which is an article from the articles of *Īmān*. The articles (pillars) of *Īmān* that have been clarified in Book of Allāh (سُبْحَانَهُوَتَعَالَ) and the Sunnah of His Messenger (صَلَّاللَّهُعَلَيْهِوَسَلَّم) are six, and from these pillars is *Īmān* in the *Qadar* (divine Pre-Decree) of Allāh and that Allāh is capable of all things; and that whatever Allāh wills, it will occur and whatever He does not wish to occur will not occur and that all affairs are under His control and disposal—there is none to put back His Judgment. None can repel His Ruling (سُبْحَانَهُوَتَعَالَ). Faith in the Divine Preordainment is indeed from the pillars of *Īmān,* and no obedience will be accepted from a servant and nor will he benefit from his deeds if he does not believe in it. Thus when Ibn 'Umar (رضي الله عنه) heard of a group of people that reject the Divine Pre-Decree, he said: "If you meet those people, inform them that I am free from them and they are free from me; and by He Who 'Abdullāh Ibn 'Umar swears by (i.e., Allāh), if one of them gave gold in charity the weight of the mountain of Uhud, Allāh would not accept it from him until he believes in the Divine Pre-Decree. "After that, he reported from his father the Long *Hadīth* of Jibrīl which makes mention of Jibrīl asking the Prophet (ﷺ) about Islām, *Īmān, Ihsān* and the Hour and its signs.[75]

So, Belief in the Divine Preordainment is one of the pillars of *Īmān* and one of the foundations of *Islām*. The example of *Īmān* is like that of the tree, which has a solid foundation; *Īmān* can only be established with a solid foundation (root). Allāh said:

$$﴿ أَلَمۡ تَرَ كَيۡفَ ضَرَبَ ٱللَّهُ مَثَلٗا كَلِمَةٗ طَيِّبَةٗ كَشَجَرَةٖ طَيِّبَةٍ أَصۡلُهَا ثَابِتٞ وَفَرۡعُهَا فِي ٱلسَّمَآءِ ۞ ﴾$$

"See you not how Allāh sets forth a parable? – A goodly word as a goodly tree, whose root is firmly fixed, and its branches (reach) to the sky (i.e., very high)." [Sūrah Ibrahim (14):24]

This is the parable for *Īmān* which Allāh set forth; it is a tree that has a firm foundation, and if its roots (its foundation) are cut off, the tree will die; similarly, *Īmān* has firm foundations, and if all or some of these foundations are gone, there will be no *Īmān* left, and this is the meaning of the statement of Allāh (تَبَارَكَ وَتَعَالَى):

---

[75] Collected in *Sahīh Muslim* (8)

﴿ وَمَن يَكْفُرْ بِٱلْإِيمَٰنِ فَقَدْ حَبِطَ عَمَلُهُ وَهُوَ فِي ٱلْأَخِرَةِ مِنَ ٱلْخَٰسِرِينَ ۝ ﴾

"And whosoever disbelieves in Faith [i.e., in the Oneness of Allāh and in all the other Articles of Faith, i.e., His (Allāh's), Angels, His Holy Books, His Messengers, the Day of Resurrection and al-Qadar (Divine Preordainments)], then fruitless is his work. In the Hereafter, he will be among the losers." [Sūrah al-Mā'idah (5):5]

And this is because *Īmān* and Islām can only be established upon these foundations from which is the belief in the Divine Pre-Decree. It has been affirmed from Ibn 'Abbās (رَضِيَٱللَّهُعَنْهُمَا) that he said: "Faith in the Divine Pre-Decree is the *Nidhām* (regulation) for *Tawhīd*; whoever believes in Allāh but denies the Divine Pre-Decree, his denial will negate his *Tawhīd*."[76] And his words are clear (رضي الله عنه وأرضاه); what he said means that denial of the Divine Pre-Decree is a denial of Faith and the *Tawhīd* of The Most Merciful (Allāh).

---

[76] Reported by 'Abdullāh Ibn al-Imām Ahmad in his book, as-*Sunnah* (3/422) and al-Lālakā'ī in *Sharh Usūl I'tiqād Ahlis-Sunnah wal-Jamā'ah* (4/742)

What will further clarify this matter is the statement of Imām Ahmad (رَحِمَهُ ٱللَّهُ): "The Divine Pre-Decree is the Ability and Power of Allāh;"[77] and Allāh (جَلَّ وَعَلَا) is capable of all things:

"Verily, Allāh can do all things." [Sūrah al-Baqarah (2):109]

So, the one who disbelieves in the Divine Predestiny disbelieves in the Power of Allāh and, as a result, disbelieves in Allāh (سُبْحَانَهُ وَتَعَالَى), and such a person is a disbeliever, he is not a Muslim. Similarly, al-Hasan al-Basrī (رَحِمَهُ ٱللَّهُ) said: "Whoever rejects the Divine Predestiny has rejected Islām."[78] So Belief in the *Qadar* is truly an important foundation from the foundations of *Īmān*. For this reason, there are many verses in the Noble *Qurʾān* that affirm this and the fact that all matters are by the Pre-Decree of Allāh (عَزَّوَجَلَّ), like His statement:

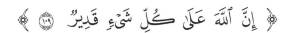

"Verily, Allāh can do all things." [Sūrah al-Baqarah (2):109]

---

[77] Reported by Ibn Hanī in his book, *Masāʾil al-Imām Ahmad* (2/155), Tahqīq of Zahīr ash-Shāwīsh.
[78] Collected by al-Lālakāʾī in *Sharh Usūl Iʾtiqād Ahlis-Sunnah wal-Jamāʾah* (4/755)

﴿ إِنَّا كُلَّ شَىْءٍ خَلَقْنَهُ بِقَدَرٍ ۝ ﴾

"**Verily, We have created all things with *Qadar* (Divine Preordainments of all things before their creation, as written in the Book of Decrees *Al-Lauh Al-Mahfuz*).**" [Sūrah al-Qamar (54):49]

And His statement:

﴿ وَكَانَ أَمْرُ ٱللَّهِ قَدَرًا مَّقْدُورًا ۝ ﴾

"**And the Command of Allāh is a decree determined.**" [Sūrah al-Ahzāb (32):38]

And His statement:

﴿ ثُمَّ جِئْتَ عَلَىٰ قَدَرٍ يَٰمُوسَىٰ ۝ ﴾

"**Then you came here according to the fixed term which I ordained (for you), O Mūsā (Moses)!**" [Sūrah Tā-Hā (20): 40]

And His statement:

﴿ سَبِّحِ ٱسْمَ رَبِّكَ ٱلْأَعْلَى ۝ ٱلَّذِى خَلَقَ فَسَوَّىٰ ۝ وَٱلَّذِى قَدَّرَ فَهَدَىٰ ۝ ﴾

"Glorify the Name of your Lord, the Most High, (1) Who has created (everything), and then proportioned it; (2) And Who has measured (preordainments for everything even to be blessed or wretched); and then guided (i.e., showed mankind the right as well as wrong paths, and guided the animals to pasture)." [Sūrah al-A'lā (87):1-3]

And His statement:

$$ \text{﴿ وَمَا تَشَاءُونَ إِلَّا أَن يَشَاءَ ٱللَّهُ رَبُّ ٱلْعَالَمِينَ ۝ ﴾} $$

"And you cannot will, unless (it be) that Allāh wills, the Lord of the *'Ālamīn* (mankind, jinn and all that exists)." [Sūrah at-Takwīr (81):29]

There are many verses like these in the Noble *Qur'ān* that affirm that all the affairs are by the Divine Preordainments of Allāh; it is He who brought this universe into existence from nothing and created the people:

$$ \text{﴿ أَلَمْ نَخْلُقكُم مِّن مَّاءٍ مَّهِينٍ ۝ فَجَعَلْنَٰهُ فِي قَرَارٍ مَّكِينٍ ۝ إِلَىٰ} $$
$$ \text{قَدَرٍ مَّعْلُومٍ ۝ فَقَدَرْنَا فَنِعْمَ ٱلْقَٰدِرُونَ ۝ ﴾} $$

"Did We not create you from despised water (semen)? Then We placed it in a place of safety (womb), For a known period (determined by gestation)? So, We did measure, and We are the Best to measure (the things)." [Sūrah al-Mursalāt (77):23]

Mankind did not exist before, Allāh brought them into existence and gave them the ability to hear, see, and granted them power and free will—this is all from the Pre-Decree of Allāh:

$$﴿ فَقَدَرْنَا فَنِعْمَ ٱلْقَٰدِرُونَ ۝ ﴾$$

"So, We did measure, and We are the Best to measure (the things)." [Sūrah al-Mursalāt (77):23]

And Allāh (جَلَّ وَعَلَا) can do all things. All things in this universe only occur by the Wish, Power, and Will of Allāh, since this universe belongs to Allāh. He deals with it as He wishes, and executes in it as He wills—none can put back His Judgments or repel His rulings:

$$﴿ مَّا يَفْتَحِ ٱللَّهُ لِلنَّاسِ مِن رَّحْمَةٍ فَلَا مُمْسِكَ لَهَا وَمَا يُمْسِكْ فَلَا مُرْسِلَ لَهُۥ مِنۢ بَعْدِهِۦ وَهُوَ ٱلْعَزِيزُ ٱلْحَكِيمُ ۝ ﴾$$

"Whatever of mercy (i.e., of good), Allāh may grant to mankind, none can withhold it, and whatever He may withhold, none can grant it after that. And He is the All-Mighty, the All-Wise." [Sūrah Fātir (35):2]

Everything is under the Predestiny of Allāh, and He (تَبَارَكَ وَتَعَالَى) is the Disposer of affairs and the One Who directs matters in this universe. So, having *Īmān* in the Divine Predestination is a great article from the articles of Faith; and *Sūrah al-Fātihah* affirms this tremendous article in many places such as:

$$\text{﴿ ٱلْحَمْدُ لِلَّهِ رَبِّ ٱلْعَٰلَمِينَ ۝ ﴾}$$

"All the praises and thanks be to Allāh, the Lord of the 'Ālamīn (mankind, jinn and all that exists)." [Sūrah al-Fātihah (1):1]

This contains your praise and exaltation for Allāh, His beautiful Names, and lofty Attributes. And from the Names of Allāh which you are praising Him for is al-Qadīr (The All-Powerful). Allāh (سُبْحَانَهُۥوَتَعَالَىٰ) is praised and thanked for His Names, Attributes, Favors, and Gifts. And from the things that you should praise and exalt Allāh for is the blessing of Faith that He has guided you to and favored you with; Allāh (سُبْحَانَهُۥوَتَعَالَىٰ) said:

$$\text{﴿ وَلَٰكِنَّ ٱللَّهَ حَبَّبَ إِلَيْكُمُ ٱلْإِيمَٰنَ وَزَيَّنَهُۥ فِى قُلُوبِكُمْ وَكَرَّهَ إِلَيْكُمُ ٱلْكُفْرَ وَٱلْفُسُوقَ وَٱلْعِصْيَانَ أُوْلَٰٓئِكَ هُمُ ٱلرَّٰشِدُونَ ۝ فَضْلًا مِّنَ ٱللَّهِ وَنِعْمَةً ﴾}$$

"But Allāh has endeared the Faith to you and has beautified it in your hearts, and has made disbelief, wickedness, and disobedience (to Allāh and His Messenger صَلَّى ٱللَّهُ عَلَيْهِ وَسَلَّمَ) hateful to you. Such are they who are the rightly guided, (This is) a Grace from Allāh and His Favor." [Sūrah al-Hujurāt (49):7-8]

So, your guidance to Faith is a Grace from Allāh:

﴿ وَلَوْلَا فَضْلُ ٱللَّهِ عَلَيْكُمْ وَرَحْمَتُهُۥ مَا زَكَىٰ مِنكُم مِّنْ أَحَدٍ أَبَدًا وَلَٰكِنَّ ٱللَّهَ يُزَكِّي مَن يَشَآءُ ﴾

"And had it not been for the Grace of Allāh and His Mercy on you, not one of you would ever have been pure from sins. But Allāh purifies (guides to Islām) whom He wills." [Sūrah an-Nūr (24):21]

﴿ يَمُنُّونَ عَلَيْكَ أَنْ أَسْلَمُوٓا۟ قُل لَّا تَمُنُّوا۟ عَلَىَّ إِسْلَٰمَكُم بَلِ ٱللَّهُ يَمُنُّ عَلَيْكُمْ أَنْ هَدَىٰكُمْ لِلْإِيمَٰنِ إِن كُنتُمْ صَٰدِقِينَ ۝ ﴾

"They regard as a favor to you (O Muḥammad ﷺ) that they have embraced Islām. Say: "Count not your Islām as a favor to me. Nay, but Allāh has conferred a favor upon you that He has guided you to the Faith if you indeed are true." [Sūrah al-Ḥujurāt (49):17]

Ēman is truly a favor from Allāh:

﴿ وَلَوْلَا فَضْلُ ٱللَّهِ عَلَيْكُمْ وَرَحْمَتُهُۥ لَٱتَّبَعْتُمُ ٱلشَّيْطَٰنَ إِلَّا قَلِيلًا ۝ ﴾

"Had it not been for the Grace and Mercy of Allāh upon you, you would have followed Shayṭān (Satan), save a few of you." [Sūrah an-Nisā (4):83]

And the entirety of the matter is for Allāh. When you recite:

$$ \text{﴿ ٱلْحَمْدُ لِلَّهِ رَبِّ ٱلْعَٰلَمِينَ ۝ ﴾} $$

"All the praises and thanks are for Allāh." [Sūrah al-Fātihah (1):1]

You are praising and exalting Allāh for His Names, Attributes, Greatness, and Magnificence; as well as His Complete Power, Tremendous Will and His directing and managing of affairs in this universe—thus 'al-Hamd' (the praise and exaltation of Allāh) contains Faith in the Divine Pre-Decree.

And in His statement:

$$ \text{﴿ رَبِّ ٱلْعَٰلَمِينَ ۝ ﴾} $$

"...The Lord of the 'Ālamīn (mankind, jinn and all that exists)." [Sūrah al-Fātihah (1):1]

It similarly contains Faith in the Divine Pre-Decree, because Belief in the Divine Pre-Decree is necessitated by Belief in the Lordship of Allāh; when you say:

$$ \text{﴿ رَبِّ ٱلْعَٰلَمِينَ ۝ ﴾} $$

"The Lord of the 'Ālamīn (mankind, jinn & all that exists)," you have believed that Allāh (عَزَّوَجَلَّ) is the Lord of all that exists and in all the meanings that the Lordship of Allāh entails; and from these meanings is: [Allāh's exclusive acts of] creating, sustaining and providing, disposing of affairs and directing and giving life and death. And when you read:

$$\text{﴿ ٱلرَّحۡمَٰنِ ٱلرَّحِيمِ ۝ ﴾}$$

The Most Gracious, the Most Merciful [Sūrah al-Fātihah (1): 2], this also contains the belief in the Divine Pre-Decree because you are hoping for Allāh's mercy; and through this hope, you recognize that you are desperately in need of Allāh and His Guidance, Grace, Gifts, Favors, and Mercy—you cannot be without Him for a blink of an eye. Also, when you recite:

$$\text{﴿ وَإِيَّاكَ نَسۡتَعِينُ ﴾}$$

"And You (Alone) we ask for help (for each and everything)." **[Sūrah al-Fātihah (1):4],** it likewise contains Belief in the Divine Pre-Decree; you are seeking help from Allāh because He is the One Who is capable of all things; you seek His aid because in His Hands is the reigns of all things and He (تَبَارَكَ وَتَعَالَى) does with His creation what He pleases. Your statement:

$$\text{﴿ ٱهۡدِنَا ٱلصِّرَٰطَ ٱلۡمُسۡتَقِيمَ ۝ ﴾}$$

"Guide us to the Straight Way" [Sūrah al-Fātihah (1):5], also contains Belief in the Divine Pre-Decree because you are requesting guidance from the One Who in His Hands is guidance, Allāh (سُبْحَانَهُ وَتَعَالَى) said to His Prophet (صَلَّى ٱللَّهُ عَلَيۡهِ وَسَلَّمَ):

$$\left\{ \text{إِنَّكَ لَا تَهْدِى مَنْ أَحْبَبْتَ وَلَكِنَّ ٱللَّهَ يَهْدِى مَن يَشَآءُ} \right\}$$

"Verily! You (O Muḥammad ﷺ) guide not whom you like, but Allāh guides whom He wills." [Sūrah al-Qasas (28): 56][79]

And He said to him:

$$\left\{ \text{۞ لَّيْسَ عَلَيْكَ هُدَاهُمْ} \right\}$$

"Not upon you (Muḥammad ﷺ) is their guidance." [Sūrah al-Baqarah (2):272]

And He (سُبْحَانَهُ وَتَعَالَى) said:

$$\left\{ \text{أَفَمَن زُيِّنَ لَهُ سُوءُ عَمَلِهِ فَرَءَاهُ حَسَنًا فَإِنَّ ٱللَّهَ يُضِلُّ مَن يَشَآءُ} \right.$$
$$\left. \text{وَيَهْدِى مَن يَشَآءُ فَلَا تَذْهَبْ نَفْسُكَ عَلَيْهِمْ حَسَرَٰتٍ} \right\}$$

"Is he, then, to whom the evil of his deeds made fair-seeming, so that he considers it as good (equal to one who is rightly guided)? Verily, Allāh sends astray whom He wills and guides whom He wills. So, don't destroy yourself

---

[79] It was revealed regarding the death of Abū Ṭālib (the Uncle of Prophet (ﷺ) who died upon disbelief) and it was reported by al-Bukhārī (4772) and Muslim (24)

(O Muḥammad ﷺ) in sorrow for them." [Sūrah Fāṭir (35):8]

And when the Prophet (عَلَيْهِ ٱلصَّلَاةُ وَٱلسَّلَامُ) would give a sermon to the people, he would say:

إِنَّ الْحَمْدَ لِلَّهِ نَحْمَدُهُ وَنَسْتَعِينُهُ وَنَسْتَغْفِرُه , مَنْ يَهْدِهِ اللهُ فَلَا مُضِلَّ لَهُ وَمَنْ يُضْلِلْ فَلَا هَادِيَ لَهُ.

"All praise and thanks are due to Allāh; we seek His Help, and we seek His Forgiveness. Whosoever Allāh guides, then none can misguide him, and whosoever Allāh leaves to stray, then none can guide him."[80]

And it has come in the long *Hadīth* of Abū Dhar that Allāh (سُبْحَانَهُ وَتَعَالَى) says:

يَا عِبَادِي كُلُّكُمْ ضَالٌّ إِلَّا مَنْ هَدَيْتُهُ، فَاسْتَهْدُونِي أَهْدِكُمْ

"O My servants, all of you are liable to err except one whom I guide on the right path, so seek guidance from Me so that I should direct you to the right path."[81]

Meaning: "Seek guidance from Me, and I will grant you success to walk on its Path." And our Prophet (عَلَيْهِ ٱلصَّلَاةُ وَٱلسَّلَامُ) use to urge his

---

[80] Reported by Muslim (868)
[81] Reported by Muslim (2577)

Companions to request guidance from Allāh, like his advice to ʿAlī (ﷺ): "Say:

$$اللَّهُمَّ اهْدِنِي وَسَدِّدْنِي$$

ʿO Allāh, guide me and grant me steadfastness upon the Straight Path.'"[82]

And his statement:

$$اللَّهُمَّ إِنِي أَسْأَلُكَ الهُدى وَالتُّقى وَالعَفَافَ وَالغِنَى$$

"O Allāh, I ask You for guidance, piety, chastity, and self-sufficiency."[83]

And his statement regarding the supplication made in the night prayer:

$$اللَّهُمَّ اهْدِنِي فِيمَنْ هَدَيْتَ$$

"O Allāh, guide me among those whom You have guided."[84]

---

[82] Reported by Muslim (2725)
[83] Reported by Muslim (2721)
[84] Reported by Abū Dāwūd (1452) and authenticated by al-Albānī (رَحِمَهُ‎اللَّه) in *Saḥīḥ Sunan Abī Dāwūd* (1/392)

Also, it has been affirmed that He (صلوات الله وسلامه عليه) use to say in his supplication:

اللَّهُمَّ لَكَ أَسْلَمْتُ وَبِكَ آمَنْتُ وَعَلَيْكَ تَوَكَّلْتُ وَإِلَيْكَ أَنَبْتُ وَبِكَ خَاصَمْتُ اللَّهُمَّ إِنِّي أَعُوذُ بِعِزَّتِكَ لاَ إِلَهَ إِلاَّ أَنْتَ أَنْ تُضِلَّنِي أَنْتَ الْحَيُّ الَّذِي لاَ يَمُوتُ وَالْجِنُّ وَالإِنْسُ يَمُوتُونَ

"O Allāh, it is unto You that I surrender myself. I affirm my faith in You and repose my trust in You and turn to You in repentance and with Your help fought my adversaries. O Allāh, I seek refuge in You with Your Power—there is no God worthy of worship but You—that you lead me astray. You are the Ever-Living that never dies, while the Jinn and mankind die."[85]

And he (عَلَيْهِ الصَّلَاةُ وَالسَّلَامُ) said:

لِلّهُمَّ مُصَرِّف القُلُوب صَرِّف قُلُوبَنا عَلى طَاعتك

"O Allāh! Controller of the hearts, direct our hearts to Your obedience."[86]

And the supplication he used to make most was:

---

[85] Reported by al-Bukhārī (7383) and Muslim (2717) and this is his wording.
[86] Reported by Muslim (2654)

يَا مُقَلِّبَ القُلُوب ثَبِّت قَلبِي عَلى دِينِك

"O Controller of the hearts, make my heart steadfast in Your religion."[87]

In the same way, your recitation of:

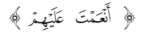

﴾ أَنْعَمْتَ عَلَيْهِمْ ﴿

"...On whom You have bestowed Your Grace," [Sūrah al-Fātihah (1):6] shows your Faith in the fact that all favors and blessings are from Allāh, whether it is the favor of health, wealth, guidance to fulfill acts of worship and belief. Therefore, this *Sūrah* encompasses and affirms the concept of Belief in the Divine Predestination from many angles. And the Muslim who regularly repeats this and is conscious of its meanings and believes in its directives; must believe in the Divine Pre-Decree and that all affairs are under the Power of Allāh: What He wills will occur and what he doesn't will won't occur, and there is no might or power except with Allāh, the Exalted, The Magnificent.

It behooves every Muslim to know the importance of having faith in the Divine Pre-Decree and its elevated status; as well as the tremendous benefits it reaps for the servant in his religion and worldly-life: It grants the heart strength, trust in Allāh, a good relationship with Him, devotion and turning to His obedience; and

---

[87] Reported by at-Tirmidhī (3522) and authenticated by al-Albānī (رَحِمَهُ اللهُ) in *Sahīh Sunan at-Tirmidhī* (3/447)

it likewise makes the heart realize its desperate need for Allāh and supplication to Him Alone, as well as encouraging it to trust Him Alone and seek his aid and frequently ask Him for guidance, success, and steadfastness. It similarly grants the servant strength in fulfilling acts of worship and obedience, and it increases his patience during calamities; because the one who believes in the Divine Preordainments knows that what afflicted him would not have missed him and what missed him would not have afflicted him, as Allāh (سُبْحَانَهُوَتَعَالَى) said:

$$ \text{﴾ مَآ أَصَابَ مِن مُّصِيبَةٍ إِلَّا بِإِذْنِ ٱللَّهِ ۗ وَمَن يُؤْمِنۢ بِٱللَّهِ يَهْدِ قَلْبَهُۥ ﴿} $$

"No calamity befalls, but by the Leave [i.e., Decision and Qadar (Divine Preordainments)] of Allāh, and whosoever believes in Allāh, He guides his heart [to the true Faith with certainty, i.e., what has befallen him was already written for him by Allāh from the Qadar (Divine Preordainments)]." [Sūrah at-Taghābun (64):11]

Thus, having Faith in the Divine Pre-Decree is from the means of attaining guidance for the hearts to all good, success, and elevation in this world and the next. Accordingly, the Messenger (عَلَيْهِٱلصَّلَاةُوَٱلسَّلَامُ) said:

"How wonderful is the case of a believer; it is good for him in every situation, and this applies only to a believer. If prosperity attends him, he expresses gratitude to Allāh,

and that is good for him. If adversity befalls him, he endures it patiently, and that is better for him."[88]

As such, the believer resorts to Allāh in all cases: If he is healthy and well or wealthy, he praises and thanks Allāh; and if he is ill, he is patient and invokes Allāh; and if he is poor, he supplicates to Allāh with the reported supplication from the Messenger of Allāh (صَلَّىٰ اللَّهُ عَلَيْهِ وَسَلَّمَ):

اللَّهُمَّ اكْفِنِي بِحَلالِكَ عَن حَرَامِكَ، وَأَغْنِنِي بِفَضْلِكَ عَمَّن سِوَاكَ

"O Allāh! Suffice me with what You make lawful so that I may be in no need of what You make unlawful, and enrich and suffice me by Your Grace so that I do not depend on other than You."[89]

So, he (the servant of Allāh) turns to Allāh, because he firmly believes that all matters are under His Power. Thus, it becomes evident that Belief in the Divine Pre-Decree has a blessed effect and tremendous benefits—that cannot be enumerated or counted—that rectify the servant with regards to his religion and worldly life. Conversely, if a person rejects Belief in the Divine Pre-Decree, everything will be ruined for him, he will be deprived of all good. He will draw on himself all failure, loss, and regret in this world and the Hereafter. This is among the matters that makes clear to us that

---

[88] Reported by Muslim (2999)
[89] Reported by at-Tirmidhī (3563) and authenticated by al-Albānī (رَحِمَهُ اللَّه) in *Saḥīḥ Sunan at-Tirmidhī* (3/464)

belief in the Divine Pre-Decree is a foundation that the tree of *Īmān* firmly stands upon; it will not bear fruit, blossom and ripen unless this blessed root is present. And the more a person's belief in the Divine Pre-Decree increases, the more goodness will increase and develop in him.

What is similarly befitting for us to know is that people discuss the Divine Pre-Decree in one of two ways:

The First Way: A person delves into the matters of the Divine Pre-Decree with his mere intellect and restricted thoughts while leaving the Speech of Allāh and His Messenger (ﷺ) concerning it; he puts the *Qur'ān* and the Sunnah to the side and discusses the Divine Pre-Decree and its more detailed rulings with his own intellect and thoughts and with his barren opinions—this is false and a serious error that will only lead its perpetrator to his demise, as he (جل ثناؤه) said:

$$﴿ وَذَٰلِكُمْ ظَنُّكُمُ ٱلَّذِى ظَنَنتُم بِرَبِّكُمْ أَرْدَىٰكُمْ فَأَصْبَحْتُم مِّنَ ٱلْخَٰسِرِينَ ۝ ﴾$$

"And that thought of yours which you thought about your Lord, has brought you to destruction, and you have become (this Day) of those utterly lost!" [Sūrah Fussilat (41):23]

And from this type also, is how a person discusses the matters of the Divine Pre-Decree in a way which indicates his rejection of Allāh, His Divine Pre-Decree, and its rulings—and refuge is sought with

Allāh—; for example, a person saying: "Why did Allāh do this or that and not this or that? Why did Allāh decree this and not this or that?" And indeed, Allāh has prohibited his servants from this with His statement:

$$﴿ لَا يُسْأَلُ عَمَّا يَفْعَلُ وَهُمْ يُسْأَلُونَ ۝ ﴾$$

"He cannot be questioned as to what He does, while they will be questioned." [Sūrah al-Anbiyā (21):23]

Because every atom in this universe belongs to Allāh (جَلَّ وَعَلَا) and for this reason, rejecting and opposing Allāh (تَبَارَكَ وَتَعَالَى) is from the gravest of falsehood and misguidance.

The Messenger of Allāh (صَلَّى اللهُ عَلَيْهِ وَسَلَّمَ) said:

$$إِذَا ذُكِرَ أَصْحَابِي فَأَمْسِكُوا، وَإِذَا ذُكِرَتِ النُّجُومُ فَأَمْسِكُوا، وَإِذَا ذُكِرَ الْقَدَرُ فَأَمْسِكُوا.$$

"If my Companions are mentioned, hold back, and if the stars and planets are mentioned, hold back, and if the Divine Pre-Decree is mentioned, hold back."[90]

These are three matters he (عَلَيْهِ الصَّلَاةُ وَالسَّلَامُ) ordered us to hold back concerning; the meaning of 'holding back' when the Divine Pre-

---

[90] Reported by at-Tabarānī (10448) and authenticated by al-Albānī (رَحِمَهُ اللهُ) in *Sahīh al-Jāmi'* (545)

Decree is mentioned is to refrain from delving into it with falsehood and in the impermissible way which we referred to earlier; because "the Divine Pre-Decree is the secret of Allāh (جَلَّوَعَلَا)" as some of the *Salaf* quoted. And whoever attempts to uncover this secret with his deficient intellect and weak thoughts, he will only fall into misguidance and become lost.

Hence, what is mandatory is to abstain from probing into the Divine Pre-Decree in an impermissible way; nonetheless, this does not nullify the permissibility of returning to the legislated texts concerning this topic and benefiting from them to gain knowledge about Belief in the Divine Pre-Decree under its light; this does not fall into the prohibition mentioned in his statement (صَلَّىاللَّهُعَلَيْهِوَسَلَّمَ): "**If the Divine Pre-Decree is mentioned, hold back;**" just as his statement: "**If my Companions are mentioned, hold back,**" is an order to not insult them and speak ill of them and with words that are not befitting; however, this does not prohibit us from speaking about the excellence and virtues of the Companions as was the way of the scholars of *Hadīth* in the books they authored. And Allāh (سُبْحَانَهُوَتَعَالَى) has praised those who give the Companions (رَضِيَاللَّهُعَنْهُمْ) their due rights and respect with his statement:

﴿ وَٱلَّذِينَ جَآءُو مِنۢ بَعْدِهِمْ يَقُولُونَ رَبَّنَا ٱغْفِرْ لَنَا وَلِإِخْوَٰنِنَا ٱلَّذِينَ سَبَقُونَا بِٱلْإِيمَٰنِ وَلَا تَجْعَلْ فِى قُلُوبِنَا غِلًّا لِّلَّذِينَ ءَامَنُوا۟ رَبَّنَآ إِنَّكَ رَءُوفٌ رَّحِيمٌ ۝ ﴾

"And those who came after them say: "Our Lord! Forgive our brethren who have preceded us in Faith and us, and put not in our hearts any hatred against those who have believed. Our Lord! You are indeed full of kindness, Most Merciful." [Sūrah al-Ḥashr (59):10]

As for delving into the subject of the stars and planets—which is referred to as *'Ilm at-Ta'thīr'* (The Knowledge of the Influence)—and believing in them and attributing world events to them, this is not permissible; although, what is permissible regarding astrology is using this knowledge for guidance and using the location of the stars to determine the location of the *Qiblah* (the direction we pray towards in our *Salāh*—the *Ka'bah*) and for determining routes [when journeying], as Allāh (سُبْحَانَهُوَتَعَالَى) said:

$$ \text{﴿} ۝ \text{وَبِالنَّجْمِ هُمْ يَهْتَدُونَ} \text{﴾} $$

"...And by the stars (during the night), they (mankind) guide themselves." [Sūrah an-Nahl (16):16]

On the authority of Qatādah, who said:

"Verily, Allāh (تَبَارَكَوَتَعَالَى) only created these stars for three reasons: He made them adornment for the sky and to be used as guides and as missiles to drive away the devils; and whoever uses them for other than these purposes has spoken with his own opinion, missed his portion, lost his

fortune and entered himself into that which he has no knowledge concerning."[91]

The Second Way: This is the correct, and it is that the speech of a person concerning the Divine Pre-Decree is in light of the evidence, and through this—by the will of Allāh—he will arrive at every sound speech and righteous good deed. And the texts have proven that a servant will not have Faith in the Divine Pre-Decree until he believes in its four stages or levels mentioned by the Book of Allāh (عَزَّوَجَلَّ) and the Sunnah of His Messenger (صَلَّىٱللَّهُعَلَيْهِوَسَلَّمَ):

1.   The Knowledge of Allāh: It is having Faith in Allāh's Encompassing Knowledge of what has taken place and what will come to occur, as well as what has not occurred, if it occurred, how it would it occur; for certainly, He (سُبْحَانَهُوَتَعَالَى):

$$ ﴾ ۝ وَمَا تُخۡفِى ٱلصُّدُورُ ٱلۡأَعۡيُنِ خَآئِنَةَ يَعۡلَمُ ﴿ $$

"Allāh knows the fraud of the eyes, and all that the breasts conceal." [Sūrah Ghāfir (40):19]

$$ ﴾ ۝ عِلۡمَۢا شَيۡءٍ بِكُلِّ أَحَاطَ قَدۡ ﴿ $$

"Allāh surrounds all things in (His) Knowledge." (at-Ṭalāq (65):12]

---

[91] Reported by Ibn Jarīr at-Ṭabarī (21549) with an authentic chain of narration.

﴾ ۞ ۲۸ عَدَدًا شَىْءٍ كُلَّ وَأَحْصَىٰ ﴿

"He (Allāh) keeps count of all things (i.e., He knows the exact number of everything)." [Sūrah al-Jinn (72):28]

And He (سُبْحَانَهُوَتَعَالَى) said:

﴿ يَعْلَمُ مَا يَلِجُ فِي ٱلْأَرْضِ وَمَا يَخْرُجُ مِنْهَا وَمَا يَنزِلُ مِنَ ٱلسَّمَاءِ وَمَا يَعْرُجُ فِيهَا وَهُوَ ٱلرَّحِيمُ ٱلْغَفُورُ ۞ ﴾

"He knows that which goes into the earth and that which comes forth from it, and that which descends from the heaven and that which ascends to it. And He is the Most Merciful, the Oft-Forgiving." [Sūrah Saba (34):2]

And He (سُبْحَانَهُوَتَعَالَى) said:

﴿ يَعْلَمُ مَا يَلِجُ فِي ٱلْأَرْضِ وَمَا يَخْرُجُ مِنْهَا وَمَا يَنزِلُ مِنَ ٱلسَّمَاءِ وَمَا يَعْرُجُ فِيهَا وَهُوَ مَعَكُمْ أَيْنَ مَا كُنتُمْ وَٱللَّهُ بِمَا تَعْمَلُونَ بَصِيرٌ ۞ ﴾

"He knows what goes into the earth and what comes forth from it, and what descends from the heaven and what ascends to it. And He is with you (by His Knowledge) wheresoever you may be. And Allāh is the All-Seer of what you do." [Sūrah al-Hadid (57):4]

And He (سُبْحَانَهُ وَتَعَالَى) said:

﴿ أَلَمْ تَرَ أَنَّ ٱللَّهَ يَعْلَمُ مَا فِي ٱلسَّمَوَاتِ وَمَا فِي ٱلْأَرْضِ مَا يَكُونُ مِن نَّجْوَىٰ ثَلَاثَةٍ إِلَّا هُوَ رَابِعُهُمْ وَلَا خَمْسَةٍ إِلَّا هُوَ سَادِسُهُمْ وَلَا أَدْنَىٰ مِن ذَٰلِكَ وَلَا أَكْثَرَ إِلَّا هُوَ مَعَهُمْ أَيْنَ مَا كَانُوا ثُمَّ يُنَبِّئُهُم بِمَا عَمِلُوا يَوْمَ ٱلْقِيَامَةِ إِنَّ ٱللَّهَ بِكُلِّ شَيْءٍ عَلِيمٌ ۝ ﴾

"Have you not seen that Allāh knows whatsoever is in the heavens and whatsoever is on the earth? There is no Najwa (secret counsel) of three. Still, He is their fourth (with His Knowledge, while He Himself is over the Throne, over the seventh heaven), nor of five. Still, He is their sixth (with His Knowledge), not of less than that or more, but He is with them (with His Knowledge) wheresoever they may be. Afterward, on the Day of Resurrection, He will inform them of what they did. Verily, Allāh is the All-Knower of everything." [Sūrah al-Mujādilah (58):7]

He (جَلَّ وَعَلَا) said:

﴿ وَلَوْ رُدُّوا لَعَادُوا لِمَا نُهُوا عَنْهُ ﴾

"But if they were returned (to the world), they would certainly revert to that which they were forbidden." **[Sūrah al-An'ām (6):28]**

Meaning: If the polytheists were returned to the worldly-life, they would revert to disbelief, and this will not occur (them being returned), but the Magnificent Lord (سُبْحَانَهُوَتَعَالَى) knows that this would occur if it happened; thus, He established His proof against them. He (جَلَّوَعَلَا) says:

$$\text{﴿ أَلَا يَعْلَمُ مَنْ خَلَقَ وَهُوَ اللَّطِيفُ الْخَبِيرُ ۝ ﴾}$$

"Should not He Who has created know? And He is the Most Kind and Courteous (to His slaves) All-Aware (of everything)." [Sūrah al-Mulk (67):14]

2.   **The Writing:** It is to believe that Allāh (عَزَّوَجَلَّ) wrote the measure of all the creation and the entirety of what will occur in *al-Lawh al-Mahfūdh* (The Preserved Tablet):

$$\text{﴿ وَكُلُّ شَيْءٍ فَعَلُوهُ فِي الزُّبُرِ ۝ وَكُلُّ صَغِيرٍ وَكَبِيرٍ مُّسْتَطَرٌ ۝ ﴾}$$

"And everything they have done is noted in (their) Records (of deeds). And everything, small and big, is written down (in al-Lawh al-Mahfūdh already beforehand, i.e., before it

befalls, or is done by its doer).” [Sūrah al-Qamar (54):52-53]

Thus, he (عَلَيْهِ ٱلصَّلَاةُوَٱلسَّلَامُ) said:

كَتَبَ اللَّهُ مَقَادِيرَ الْخَلَائِقِ قَبْلَ أَنْ يَخْلُقَ السَّمَوَاتِ وَالْأَرْضَ بِخَمْسِينَ أَلْفَ سَنَةٍ – قَالَ – وَعَرْشُهُ عَلَى الْمَاءِ

“Allāh wrote the measures of the creation fifty thousand years before He created the heavens and the earth, as His Throne was upon water.”[92]

And he (عَلَيْهِ ٱلصَّلَاةُوَٱلسَّلَامُ) said:

إِنَّ أَوَّلَ مَا خَلَقَ اللَّهُ الْقَلَمَ فَقَالَ لَهُ اكْتُبْ فَجَرَى بِمَا هُوَ كَائِنٌ إِلَى الْأَبَدِ

“Verily, the first of what Allāh created was the Pen. He said to it: ‘Write the Divine Predestiny, what will be forever.’”[93]

---

[92] Reported by Muslim (2653)
[93] Reported by at-Tirmidhī (2155) and authenticated by al-Albānī (رَحِمَهُٱللَّهُ) in *Sahīh Sunan at-Tirmidhī* (2/450)

So, from your belief in the Divine Pre-Decree is to believe that everything that will ever occur is written in *al-Lawh al-Mahfūdh:*

$$ \{ \text{إِنَّ ذَٰلِكَ عَلَى ٱللَّهِ يَسِيرٌ} \} $$

"Verily, it is (all) in the Book (al-Lawh al-Mahfūdh). Verily! that is easy for Allāh." [Sūrah al-Hajj (22):70]

3.   **The Will of Allāh:** To believe in the Will of Allāh (تَبَارَكَوَتَعَالَى) that cannot be overcome and in His Encompassing Power; and that whatever Allāh wishes will come to take place and what he does not wish for, will not occur; Allāh (سُبْحَانَهُوَتَعَالَى) said:

$$ \{ \text{لِمَن شَاءَ مِنكُمْ أَن يَسْتَقِيمَ ۞ وَمَا تَشَاءُونَ إِلَّا أَن يَشَاءَ ٱللَّهُ رَبُّ ٱلْعَالَمِينَ} \} $$

"To whomsoever among you who wills to walk straight, and you cannot will, unless (it be) that Allāh wills, the Lord of the 'Ālamīn (mankind, jinn and all that exists)." [Sūrah at-Takwīr (81):28-29]

Everything occurs by the Will of Allāh, and it is impossible for any movement, inactivity, life, death, descent, elevation, guidance, misguidance to take place in this universe without Allāh's Will. It was once said to a Bedouin: "How did you come to know your Lord?" He said: "Through the ending of determinations and the easing of grief." And from the most beautiful statements of the

Muslims is: "What Allāh wills to happen will occur and what He does not will to happen will not occur."

4.   **The Creation:** To believe that Allāh is the Creator of everything, as Allāh (سُبْحَانَهُوَتَعَالَى) said:

$$﴿ ۞ ٱللَّهُ خَٰلِقُ كُلِّ شَىْءٍ ۞ ﴾$$

"Allāh is the Creator of all things." [Sūrah az-Zumar (39):62]

And He (سُبْحَانَهُوَتَعَالَى) said:

$$﴿ ۞ وَٱللَّهُ خَلَقَكُمْ وَمَا تَعْمَلُونَ ۝ ۞ ﴾$$

"While Allāh has created you and what you make!" [Sūrah as-Sāffāt (37):96]

And He said in *Sūrah al-Fātihah*:

$$﴿ ۞ ٱلْحَمْدُ لِلَّهِ رَبِّ ٱلْعَٰلَمِينَ ۝ ۞ ﴾$$

"All the praises and thanks are for Allāh, the Lord of the *ʿĀlamīn* (mankind, jinn and all that exists)." [Sūrah al-Fātihah (1):1]

And the *"ʿĀlam'* is everything besides Allāh; so everything besides Allāh, He (تَبَارَكَوَتَعَالَى) created it and brought it into existence. One of the people of knowledge gathered 'The Four Levels of Belief in the Divine Pre-Decree' in a line of poetry, he said:

Knowledge and the Writing of our Master and His Will; and the Creation, which is bringing into being and occasioning.

The Prophet (ﷺ) said:

لُّ شَىْءٍ بِقَدَرٍ حَتَّى الْعَجْزِ وَالْكَيْسِ

"Everything is by Decree, even incapability and ability."[94]

And Ibn 'Abbās (رضي الله عنهما) said: "Everything is by the Divine Pre-Decree, even you placing your hand on your chin, it is by Decree." And if you believe that all matters are by the Pre-Decree of Allāh and that everything that takes place in this universe from guidance, Faith, righteousness, disbelief and other than that is by the Will of Allāh, a question might arise in your mind, a question that poses itself: Why should we do anything? And this is a question that the Prophet (ﷺ) was asked by the Companions.

On the authority of 'Alī (ﷺ) who said: "We were with the Prophet (ﷺ) in *Baqī' al-Gharqad* (a cemetery in al-Madīnah) for a funeral when he said:

مَا مِنْكُمْ مِنْ أَحَدٍ إِلاَّ وَقَدْ كُتِبَ مَقْعَدُهُ مِنَ الْجَنَّةِ وَمَقْعَدُهُ مِنَ النَّارِ ".

فَقُلْنَا يَا رَسُولَ اللَّهِ أَفَلاَ نَتَّكِلُ قَالَ " لاَ، اعْمَلُوا فَكُلٌّ مُيَسَّرٌ ". ثُمَّ قَرَأَ

$$(\text{فَأَمَّا مَنْ أَعْطَى وَاتَّقَى * وَصَدَّقَ بِالْحُسْنَى * فَسَنُيَسِّرُهُ لِلْيُسْرَى}) \text{ إِلَى قَوْلِهِ}$$

$$(\text{فَسَنُيَسِّرُهُ لِلْعُسْرَى})$$

'There is none among you but has a place assigned for him either in Paradise or in the Hell.' The Companions said: 'O Messenger of Allāh, should we not depend upon what has been written for us (and give up doing good deeds)?' The Messenger of Allāh (صَلَّى ٱللَّهُ عَلَيْهِ وَسَلَّمَ) said: 'Carry on doing good deeds. Everyone will find it easy to do the deeds (as will lead him to his destined place).' Then he read:

"As for him who gives (in charity) and keeps his duty to Allāh and fears Him, And believes in al-Husnā (Paradise). We will make smooth for him the path of ease (goodness). But he who is a greedy miser and thinks himself self-sufficient. And gives belies al-Husnā; (9) We will make smooth for him the path for evil." [Sūrah al-Layl (92):5-10]"[95]

And on the authority of 'Imrān Ibn Husayn (رضي الله عنه): "I said, 'O Messenger of Allāh, what is the use of those who do good deeds?' He said:

$$\text{اِعْمَلُوا، فَكُلٌّ مُيَسَّرٌ لِمَا خُلِقَ لَهُ}$$

---

[95] Reported by al-Bukhārī (4945) and by Muslim (2647)

'Do perform good deeds, for everyone will find it easy to do the deeds for which he has been created.'"[96]

The Prophet (ﷺ) answered his Companions with that which is illumination, light, and cure for the believers' hearts; and this is the sound answer and the true statement regarding this issue which posed itself: "Perform good deeds, for everyone will find it easy to do the deeds for which he has been created." And this answer encompassed two important principles regarding this topic—none will attain happiness without actualizing these two matters:

The First Principle: Belief in the fact that a servant has free will, as was evident from his statement (عَلَيْهِ ٱلصَّلَاةُ وَٱلسَّلَامُ): "Perform good deeds." As for the one who does not have free will, it would not be said to him, "Do something," or "Leave this." In fact, all the commandments and prohibitions in the *Qur'ān* are proof that a person has free will; and this free will was created by Allāh (جَلَّ وَعَلَا) and brought into existence for you; and thus He guided you to the two ways: The way of good and the way of evil; and He sent Messengers to you, revealed books and clarified the Path. So you know the path that will lead you to good, and you understand the way that will lead you to evil. This is why you will find a Muslim turning to performing acts of obedience and distancing himself from committing illegal actions by the *Tawfīq* of Allāh. As for the one who is forced to do something without choice, he will not be held to account due to the statement of Allāh (سُبْحَانَهُ وَتَعَالَى):

---

[96] Reported by al-Bukhārī (7551) and by Muslim (2649)

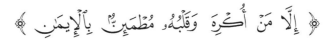

﴿ إِلَّا مَنْ أُكْرِهَ وَقَلْبُهُ مُطْمَئِنٌّ بِالْإِيمَانِ ﴾

"…Except him who is forced to that and whose heart is at rest with Faith." [Sūrah an-Nahl (16):106]

The Second Principle: Believing that all matters are by the Pre-Decree of Allāh and His Will, as is in his statement: "Everyone will find it easy to do the deeds for which he has been created."

Having *Īmān* in the Divine Pre-Decree requires two things:

First: Depending on Allāh and placing one's trust in Him, entrusting Him (سُبْحَانَهُ وَتَعَالَى) with all affairs.

Second: Taking the means; let the intelligent one reflect over the following *Ahādīth*:

اِحْرِصْ عَلَى مَا يَنْفَعُكَ, وَاسْتَعِنْ بِاللَّهِ, وَلَا تَعْجَزْ, وَإِنْ أَصَابَكَ شَيْءٌ فَلَا

تَقُلْ: لَوْ أَنِّي فَعَلْتُ كَانَ كَذَا وَكَذَا, وَلَكِنْ قُلْ: قَدَّرَ اللَّهُ وَمَا شَاءَ فَعَلَ;

فَإِنَّ لَوْ تَفْتَحُ عَمَلَ الشَّيْطَانِ

"Adhere to that which is beneficial for you. Keep asking Allāh for help, and do not refrain from it. If you are afflicted in any way, do not say: 'If I had taken this or that step, it would have resulted in such and such,' but say

only: 'Allāh so decreed it and did as He willed.' The word 'if' opens the gates of satanic thoughts."[97]

لَوْ أَنَّكُمْ كُنْتُمْ تَوَكَّلُونَ عَلَى اللَّهِ حَقَّ تَوَكُّلِهِ لَرُزِقْتُمْ كَمَا تُرْزَقُ الطَّيْرُ تَغْدُو خِمَاصًا وَتَرُوحُ بِطَانًا

"If you were to rely upon Allāh with the required reliance, then He would provide for you just as a bird is provided for, it goes out in the morning empty, and returns full."[98]

اِعْقِلْهَا وَتَوَكَّلْ

"Tie it and rely upon (Allāh)."[99]

إِنَّمَا الْعِلْمُ بِالتَّعَلُّمِ، وَالْفِقْهُ بِالتَّفَقُّهِ

"Knowledge is gained only by learning and religious understanding only through seeking its knowledge."[100]

Thus, we must understand through this great perspective that having *Īmān* in the Divine Pre-Decree requires a person to come with the

---

[97] Reported by Muslim (2664)

[98] Reported by at-Tirmidhī (2344) and authenticated by al-Albānī (رَحِمَهُاللَّه) in *Sahīh Sunan at-Tirmidhī* (2/452)

[99] Reported by at-Tirmidhī (2517) and authenticated by al-Albānī (رَحِمَهُاللَّه) in *Sahīh Sunan at-Tirmidhī* (2/610)

[100] Reported by at-Tabarānī (19/929) and deemed Hasan *Li-ghayrih* by al-Albānī (رَحِمَهُاللَّه) in *Sahīh at-Targhīb* (67)

means and strive against himself in performing good deeds; and Allāh (تَبَارَكَ وَتَعَالَى) has combined these two matters in His statement:

$$ ﴿ إِيَّاكَ نَعْبُدُ وَإِيَّاكَ نَسْتَعِينُ ۝ ﴾ $$

"You (Alone) we worship, and You (Alone) we ask for help (for each and everything)." [Sūrah al-Fātihah (1):4]

And in His statement:

$$ ﴿ فَاعْبُدْهُ وَتَوَكَّلْ عَلَيْهِ ﴾ $$

"So, worship Him (O Muḥammad صَلَّى اللَّهُ عَلَيْهِ وَسَلَّمَ) and put your trust in Him." [Sūrah Hūd (11):123]

And in His statement:

$$ ﴿ لِمَن شَاءَ مِنكُمْ أَن يَسْتَقِيمَ ۝ وَمَا تَشَاءُونَ إِلَّا أَن يَشَاءَ اللَّهُ رَبُّ الْعَالَمِينَ ۝ ﴾ $$

"To whomsoever among you who wills to walk straight, (28) And you cannot will, unless (it be) that Allāh wills, the Lord of the *'Ālamīn* (mankind, jinn and all that exists)." [Sūrah at-Takwīr (81):28-29]

And *Tawfīq* is solely in the Hands of Allāh; I place my trust in Him and turn back to Him.

8ᵀᴴ GUIDELINE: CLARIFICATION OF THE STATUS OF DUAA (SUPPLICATION)

Indeed, from the magnificent and blessed directives that we gain from *Sūrah al-Fātihah* is the clarification of the status of *Du'ā,* its importance and the Muslim's dire need for it at all times; as well as a clear explanation of the etiquettes and conditions of *Du'ā* and the praiseworthy attributes and manners that the one supplicating should adorn himself with.

As for the clarification of the significance of *Du'ā* in *Sūrah al-Fātihah*, the core of the entire *Sūrah* is a supplication to Allāh (جَلَّوَعَلَا), a request from Him and humbleness to Him; and it is the opening chapter of the *Qur'ān*. The Book of Allāh starts with a *Du'ā* just as it concludes with a *Du'ā*; because the last *Sūrah* in the *Qur'ān* is *Sūrah an-Nās* and it is likewise a supplication to Allāh (جَلَّوَعَلَا). And this is from the clearest proofs and the most brilliant of clarifications regarding the importance of *Du'ā* and its high status; in addition to the numerous verses in the Book of Allāh (جَلَّوَعَلَا) and *Ahādīth* of His Prophet (صَلَّاللَّهُعَلَيْهِوَسَلَّمَ) that similarly explain its great virtue and that it is a symbol of goodness, a fundamental element of success, true happiness and the key to every good in this world and the Hereafter. Allāh (سُبْحَانَهُوَتَعَالَى) said:

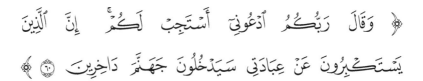

"And your Lord said: "Invoke Me, [i.e., believe in My Oneness (Islāmic Monotheism)] (and ask Me for anything) I will respond to your (invocation). Verily! Those who scorn My worship [i.e., do not invoke Me, and do not believe in My Oneness, (Islāmic Monotheism)] they will surely enter Hell in humiliation!" [Sūrah Ghāfir (40):60]

And He (سُبْحَانَهُوَتَعَالَى) said:

﴿ إِنَّ رَبِّى لَسَمِيعُ ٱلدُّعَآءِ ٣٩ ﴾

"Verily! My Lord is indeed the All-Hearer of invocations." [Sūrah Ibrāhīm (14):39]

And He (سُبْحَانَهُوَتَعَالَى) said:

﴿ ٱدْعُواْ رَبَّكُمْ تَضَرُّعًا وَخُفْيَةً إِنَّهُ لَا يُحِبُّ ٱلْمُعْتَدِينَ ٥٥ وَلَا تُفْسِدُواْ فِى ٱلْأَرْضِ بَعْدَ إِصْلَٰحِهَا وَٱدْعُوهُ خَوْفًا وَطَمَعًا إِنَّ رَحْمَتَ ٱللَّهِ قَرِيبٌ مِّنَ ٱلْمُحْسِنِينَ ٥٦ ﴾

"Invoke your Lord with humility and in secret. He likes not the aggressors. And do not make mischief on the earth, after it has been set in order, and invoke Him with fear

and hope; Surely, Allāh's Mercy is (ever) near unto the good-doers." [Sūrah al-A'rāf (7):55-56]

And He (سُبْحَانَهُوَتَعَالَى) said:

$$﴿ وَإِذَا سَأَلَكَ عِبَادِى عَنِّى فَإِنِّى قَرِيبٌ أُجِيبُ دَعْوَةَ ٱلدَّاعِ إِذَا دَعَانِ فَلْيَسْتَجِيبُواْ لِى وَلْيُؤْمِنُواْ بِى لَعَلَّهُمْ يَرْشُدُونَ ۝ ﴾$$

"And when My slaves ask you (O Muḥammad صَلَّىاللهُعَلَيْهِوَسَلَّمَ) concerning Me, then (answer them), I am indeed near (to them by My Knowledge). I respond to the invocations of the supplicant when he calls on Me (without any mediator or intercessor). So, let them obey Me and believe in Me so that they may be led aright." [Sūrah al-Baqarah (2):186]

And He (سُبْحَانَهُوَتَعَالَى) said:

$$﴿ مَا عِندَكُمْ يَنفَدُ وَمَا عِندَ ٱللَّهِ بَاقٍ ﴾$$

"Whatever is with you, will be exhausted, and whatever is with Allāh (of good deeds) will remain." [Sūrah an-Nahl (16):96]

And the Messenger of Allāh (صَلَّىاللهُعَلَيْهِوَسَلَّمَ) said:

يَدُ اللهِ مَلأَى لاَ تَغِيضُهَا نَفَقَةٌ، سَحَاءُ اللَّيْلَ وَالنَهَارَ

"Allāh's Hand is full, and (its fullness) is not affected by the continuous spending, day and night."[101]

And He (صَلَّىٱللَّهُعَلَيهِوَسَلَّمَ) reported that Allāh (تَبَارَكَوَتَعَالَى) said:

يَا عِبَادِي لَوْ أَنَّ أَوَّلَكُمْ وَآخِرَكُمْ وَإِنْسَكُمْ وَجِنَّكُمْ قَامُوا فِي صَعِيدٍ وَاحِدٍ فَسَأَلُونِي فَأَعْطَيْتُ كُلَّ إِنْسَانٍ مَسْأَلَتَهُ مَا نَقَصَ ذَلِكَ مِمَّا عِنْدِي إِلاَّ كَمَا يَنْقُصُ الْمِخْيَطُ إِذَا أُدْخِلَ الْبَحْرَ

"O My servants, even if the first amongst you and the last amongst you and the whole human race of yours and that of Jinns also all stand in one plain ground and you ask Me and I confer upon every person what he asks for, it would not cause any loss to Me in any way (even less) than that which is caused to the ocean by dipping the needle in it."[102]

And He (صَلَّىٱللَّهُعَلَيهِوَسَلَّمَ) said:

لَيْسَ شَيْءٌ أَكْرَمَ عَلَى اللَّهِ تَعَالَى مِنَ الدُّعَاءِ

---

[101] Reported by al-Bukhāri (4684) and Muslim (993)
[102] Reported by Muslim (2577)

"There is nothing nobler to Allāh (سُبْحَانَهُوَتَعَالَى) than supplication."[103]

And He (صَلَّىاللَّهُعَلَيْهِوَسَلَّمَ) said:

مَنْ لَمْ يَسْأَلِ اللَّهَ يَغْضَبْ عَلَيْهِ

"Whoever does not supplicate to Allāh, He will become angry with Him."[104]

Allāh (عَزَّوَجَلَّ) will become angry with His servant if he abandons supplicating to Him; because the servant will begin to feel that he is in no need of his Lord (سُبْحَانَهُوَتَعَالَى), and this is from the frailty of one's worship and weakness of his religion. As for the one whose religion becomes refined, his belief strong and his relationship with his Lord firm, he will hold fast to the *Du'ā* of Allāh and frequently invoke Him (تَبَارَكَوَتَعَالَى) for well-being in his religion, worldly life, and Hereafter. These matters cannot be rectified and refined for the servant except through Allāh's facilitation, success, and reformation. Due to this, the Prophet (صَلَّىاللَّهُعَلَيْهِوَسَلَّمَ) use to supplicate with the following:

---

[103] Reported by at-Tirmidhī (3370) and graded *Hasan* by al-Albānī (رَحِمَهُاللَّه) in *Sahih Sunan at-Tirmidhī* (3/383)

[104] Reported by at-Tirmidhī (3373) and graded *Hasan* by al-Albānī (رَحِمَهُاللَّه) in *Sahih Sunan at-Tirmidhī* (3/384)

اللَّهُمَّ أَصْلِحْ لِي دِينِي الَّذِي هُوَ عِصْمَةُ أَمْرِي وَأَصْلِحْ لِي دُنْيَايَ الَّتِي فِيهَا

مَعَاشِي وَأَصْلِحْ لِي آخِرَتِي الَّتِي فِيهَا مَعَادِي وَاجْعَلْ الْحَيَاةَ زِيَادَةً لِي فِي كُلِّ

خَيْرٍ وَاجْعَلْ الْمَوْتَ رَاحَةً لِي مِنْ كُلِّ شَرٍّ

"O Allāh, rectify my religion for me, which is the safeguard of my affairs; and rectify my worldly (affairs), wherein is my livelihood; and rectify my afterlife to which is my return; and make my life for me (as a means) for an increase in every good and make death (for me) as a rest from every evil."[105]

Everything is in His (سُبْحَانَهُوَتَعَالَى) hands, and this is why one of the Salaf made an astonishing statement regarding this topic: "I pondered over the affair, and I came to the realization that its beginning is from Allāh and its end is to Allāh, and everything in it is from Allāh; there is no movement or inactivity, or standing or sitting or anything else except that is from Allāh. So I realized from this that the key to all good is Du'ā (supplication) to Allāh."

The Prophet (صَلَّىاللهُعَلَيْهِوَسَلَّمَ) said:

يُسْتَجَابُ لِأَحَدِكُمْ مَا لَمْ يَعْجَلْ يَقُولُ دَعَوْتُ فَلَمْ يُسْتَجَبْ لِي

---

[105] Reported by Muslim (2720)

"The supplication of every one of you is answered so long as he does not grow impatient and say: 'I supplicated, but it was not granted.'"[106]

And He (جَلَّ وَعَلَا) loves that His slave persistently calls upon Him and increases in humbling himself in front of Him, contrary to the people, who get irritated with the one who persistently asks them for something and begin to actively dislike him; thus, it was said: "Allāh becomes angry if you abandon supplicating to him, and the children of Adam become angry when asked for something."

And whoever looks into the Sunnah of the noble Prophet (صَلَّى ٱللَّهُ عَلَيْهِ وَسَلَّمَ)—our role model and example—will become familiar with the high status of *Du'ā*; because he (عَلَيْهِ ٱلصَّلَاةُ وَٱلسَّلَامُ) was the one who was most in supplicating to Allāh from the people, the best in being hopeful and the most complete in worship; and he was the most humble and highest in showing his desperateness in front of Allāh (جَلَّ وَعَلَا). He used to frequently invoke Allāh and remember Him at all times. It has been reported from him (عَلَيْهِ ٱلصَّلَاةُ وَٱلسَّلَامُ) words of remembrance and supplications to be said during the day and night: in the morning and evening, at the time of sleep, at the conclusion of the daily prayers, inside the prayers, when leaving and entering the home, at the onset and completion of eating food and when boarding a means of transport. And He (عَلَيْهِ ٱلصَّلَاةُ وَٱلسَّلَامُ) used to

---

[106] Reported by al-Bukhārī (6340) and Muslim (2735)

supplicate to Allāh with concise and complete supplications as has been mentioned by 'Āishah (رَضِيَاللَّهُعَنْهَا):

انَ رَسُولُ اللَّهِ صلى الله عليه وسلم يَسْتَحِبُّ الْجَوَامِعَ مِنَ الدُّعَاءِ وَيَدَعُ
مَا سِوَى ذَلِكَ

"The Messenger of Allāh (صَلَّىاللَّهُعَلَيْهِوَسَلَّمَ) used to favor the concise and comprehensive supplications and leave off other than them."[107]

And the supplications with which he (صَلَّىاللَّهُعَلَيْهِوَسَلَّمَ) used to supplicate to his Lord are complete and protected supplications that are free from mistakes and errors because he as His Lord (سُبْحَانَهُوَتَعَالَى) said:

﴿ وَمَا يَنطِقُ عَنِ ٱلْهَوَىٰٓ ۝ إِنْ هُوَ إِلَّا وَحْىٌ يُوحَىٰ ۝ ﴾

"Nor does he speak of (his own) desire. (3) It is only a Revelation revealed." [Sūrah an-Najm (53):3-4]

And they contain the most complete of requests, honorable desires, and noble goals without any faults, slipups, and mistakes. As for other than his supplications (عَلَيْهِالصَّلَاةُوَالسَّلَامُ), they are not safe and do not guarantee security, rather, some of the innovations of the people contain *Shirk* with Allāh (acts of polytheism) and severe

---

[107] Reported by Abū Dāwūd (1482) and authenticated by al-Albānī (رَحِمَهُاللَّهُ) in *Sahīh Sunan Abī Dāwūd* (1/408)

innovations; or they might contain impermissible wordings or just weakness in their form and expression. And such supplications might be safe; however, the supplications that the Messenger of Allāh (ﷺ) used are more upright and complete. Thus, the people of knowledge consider from the clearest of mistakes and acts of misguidance is the formation of supplications by some of the people or their scholars that are written on paper and then read in the morning and evening, at the conclusion of the daily prayers and at the time of sleep, while abandoning the protected supplications of the Prophet (ﷺ); where are these people with regards to following and emulating the Messenger (عليه الصلاة والسلام) and venerating what he has come with? And they claim to love him? Allāh (سبحانه وتعالى) says:

﴿ قُلْ إِن كُنتُمْ تُحِبُّونَ ٱللَّهَ فَٱتَّبِعُونِى يُحْبِبْكُمُ ٱللَّهُ وَيَغْفِرْ لَكُمْ ذُنُوبَكُمْ وَٱللَّهُ غَفُورٌ رَّحِيمٌ ۝ ﴾

"Say (O Muḥammad ﷺ to mankind): "If you (really) love Allāh then follow me (i.e., accept Islāmic Monotheism, follow the *Qur'ān* and the Sunnah), Allāh will love you and forgive you your sins. And Allāh is Oft-Forgiving, Most Merciful." [Sūrah Āli 'Imrān (3):31]

You might find in the hands of some of the people a *Wird* (an allocated reading) of such and such. It contains some matters that have not been affirmed in the Sunnah or reported from the Messenger (عليه الصلاة والسلام), but it was instead made up by one of "the scholars. "Then to disburse and propagate it amongst some of the laymen, these made up readings of certain statements guarantee a false dream; so the one who formed this special reading would say: "After I completed writing this special *Wird*, I saw the Prophet (ﷺ) in a dream," or, "I saw Abū Bakr and 'Umar in a dream," or something like this. Then he would say: "The Prophet (ﷺ) said to me: 'This is a blessed and beneficial *Wird*, spread it amongst the nation; Allāh will benefit others through it.' If it was not for this dream, I would not have spread it amongst the people." And the laymen believe this while this *Wird* contains *Shirk*, innovations, and errors; and indeed, the Prophet (ﷺ) said:

$$إِنَّ أَخْوَفَ مَا أَخَافُ عَلَيْكُمُ الْأَئِمَّةُ الْمُضِلُّونَ$$

"Indeed, what I fear most for my nation is those leaders who will lead others astray."[108]

ash-Shātibī (رحمه الله) said: "Dreams are for glad tidings and warnings, not to establish rulings." Rulings are not taken from dreams and nor is one's religion based on dreams, just as it is not based on experience like some claim: "Such and such supplication has been tried by so and so." Some went as far as claiming that supplicating to the graves has been tried and that it contains many benefits; they say: "The grave of so and so is a time-tested & proven remedy."

Like this, they misguide and turn the people away—with the likes of these false statements, dreams, stories, and fables—from the

---

[108] Reported by Ahmad (6/441) and authenticated by al-Albānī (رحمه الله) in *Sahīh al-Jāmi'* (1551)

religion of Allāh (تَبَارَكَوَتَعَالَى) and from what they should be doing like making *Du'ā* to Him and *Dhikr* (the legislated remembrance of Allāh (سُبْحَانَهُوَتَعَالَى)). It is incumbent upon the Muslim to be aware and cautious of this matter and to turn to the supplications of the noble Messenger (صَلَّىاللهُعَلَيْهِوَسَلَّمَ).

Sūrah al-Fātihah comprises several conditions and etiquettes for making *Du'ā* which will cause a believer's supplication to be answered, and his hopes fulfilled, and request granted if he adorns himself with them and fulfills them:

1.   **Sincerity (*al-Ikhlās*):** To be sincere to Allāh (تَبَارَكَوَتَعَالَى) Alone Du'ā. This is the greatest condition and its mentioned before this supplication in *Sūrah al-Fātihah*:

$$ \text{﴿ اهْـدِنَا الصِّرَاطَ الْمُسْتَقِيمَ ۝ ﴾} $$

"Guide us to the Straight Way." [Sūrah al-Fātihah (1):6]

From the conditions for the acceptance of supplications is being sincere to Allāh. Still, if this [act of worship] is directed towards other than Allāh or if it is directed to a partner made alongside Allāh, then it will be void and rejected. Thus, Allāh (سُبْحَانَهُوَتَعَالَى) said:

$$ \text{﴿ وَمَنْ أَضَلُّ مِمَّن يَدْعُواْ مِن دُونِ اللَّهِ مَن لَّا يَسْتَجِيبُ لَهُ} $$
$$ \text{إِلَىٰ يَوْمِ الْقِيَٰمَةِ وَهُمْ عَن دُعَآئِهِمْ غَٰفِلُونَ ۝ وَإِذَا حُشِرَ النَّاسُ} $$
$$ \text{كَانُوا لَهُمْ أَعْدَآءً وَكَانُوا بِعِبَادَتِهِمْ كَٰفِرِينَ ۝ ﴾} $$

"And who is more astray than one who calls on (invokes) besides Allāh, such as will not answer him till the Day of Resurrection, and who are (even) unaware of their calls (invocations) to them? And when mankind are gathered (on the Day of Resurrection), they (false deities) will become their enemies and will deny their worshipping." [Sūrah al-Aḥqāf (46):5-6]

And He (تَبَارَكَ وَتَعَالَى) said:

﴿ وَٱلَّذِينَ تَدْعُونَ مِن دُونِهِۦ مَا يَمْلِكُونَ مِن قِطْمِيرٍ ۝ إِن تَدْعُوهُمْ لَا يَسْمَعُواْ دُعَآءَكُمْ وَلَوْ سَمِعُواْ مَا ٱسْتَجَابُواْ لَكُمْ وَيَوْمَ ٱلْقِيَٰمَةِ يَكْفُرُونَ بِشِرْكِكُمْ وَلَا يُنَبِّئُكَ مِثْلُ خَبِيرٍ ۝ ﴾

"And those, whom you invoke or call upon instead of Him, own not even a Qiṭmīr (the thin membrane over the date-stone). If you invoke (or call upon) them, they hear not your call, and if (in case) they were to hear, they could not grant it (your request) to you. And on the Day of Resurrection, they will disown your worship of them. And none can inform you (O Muḥammad صَلَّى ٱللَّهُ عَلَيْهِ وَسَلَّمَ) like Him Who is the All-Knower (of everything)." [Sūrah Fāṭir (35): 13-14]

And the Prophet (صَلَّى ٱللَّهُ عَلَيْهِ وَسَلَّمَ) said:

يَا فَاطِمَةُ بِنْتَ مُحَمَّدٍ سَلِينِي مَا شِئْتِ لاَ أُغْنِي عَنْكِ مِنَ اللهِ شَيْئًا

"O Fāṭimah, daughter of Muḥammad, ask me for whatever you like, but I cannot avail you at all against Allāh."[109]

If a person says: "I would love for the Messenger of Allāh (صَلَّىٰاللَّهُعَلَيْهِوَسَلَّمَ) to intercede on my behalf." The answer to that is: "Every Muslim would love for the Messenger (صَلَّىٰاللَّهُعَلَيْهِوَسَلَّمَ) to intercede for him. However, this is not sought from him (عَلَيْهِٱلصَّلَاةُوَٱلسَّلَامُ), it is sought from Allāh. This is why when Abū Hurairah (رَضِيَاللَّهُعَنْهُ) asked the Prophet (عَلَيْهِٱلصَّلَاةُوَٱلسَّلَامُ):

لَقَدْ ظَنَنْتُ يَا أَبَا هُرَيْرَةَ أَنْ لاَ يَسْأَلَنِي عَنْ هَذَا الْحَدِيثِ أَحَدٌ أَوَّلُ مِنْكَ، لِمَا رَأَيْتُ مِنْ حِرْصِكَ عَلَى الْحَدِيثِ، أَسْعَدُ النَّاسِ بِشَفَاعَتِي يَوْمَ الْقِيَامَةِ مَنْ قَالَ لاَ إِلَهَ إِلاَّ اللَّهُ، خَالِصًا مِنْ قَلْبِهِ أَوْ نَفْسِهِ

"O Messenger of Allāh, who will be the fortunate person who will gain your intercession on the Day of Resurrection? Allāh's Messenger (صَلَّىٰاللَّهُعَلَيْهِوَسَلَّمَ) said: 'O Abū Hurairah! I have thought that none will ask me about it before you as I know your longing for the (learning of) Hadīth. The fortunate person who will have my intercession on the Day of Resurrection will be the one who

---

said sincerely from the bottom of his heart 'None has the right to be worshipped but Allāh.'"[110]

The prophets are intermediaries between Allāh and His creation for clarifying the religion. They are not intermediaries between Allāh and His creation for supplications and acts of worship to be made to them. Whoever analyzes numerous verses of the Noble *Qur'ān* will find that many verses begin with:

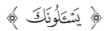

"They ask you (O Muḥammad (ﷺ))." [Sūrah n-Nāzi'āt: 42)

And the answer to their questioning will come as:

"Say (O Muḥammad (ﷺ))." [Sūrah Āli 'Imrān (3):31]

So, the Prophet (ﷺ) would then be the intermediary for conveying the religion; however, in the context of *Du'ā*, this mediation is lifted, and the answer comes directly from Allāh:

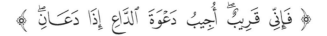

---

[110] Reported by al-Bukhārī (99)

"I am indeed near (to them by My Knowledge). I respond to the invocations of the supplicant when he calls on Me (without any mediator or intercessor)." [Sūrah al-Baqarah (2):186]

As for the belief that an invocation is more beneficial or likely to be accepted near the grave of so and so, or when you bring a picture of the 'Shaykh' and look at it and what is similar to this from people's clinging to things; this is all clear misguidance.

2.   **Compliance (al-Mutāba'ah)** with the way of the Noble Messenger (صَلَّى ٱللَّهُ عَلَيْهِ وَسَلَّمَ). This is also found in *Sūrah al-Fātihah* in His statement:

﴿ ٱهۡدِنَا ٱلصِّرَٰطَ ٱلۡمُسۡتَقِيمَ ۝ ﴾

"Guide us to the Straight Way." [Sūrah al-Fātihah (1):6]

Meaning: The upright way and the righteous path that our Prophet (صَلَّى ٱللَّهُ عَلَيْهِ وَسَلَّمَ) was firm upon. Shaykh al-Islām Ibn Taymiyyah (رَحِمَهُ ٱللَّهُ) said: "It is a must for the creation to supplicate with the legislated supplications mentioned in the Book and the Sunnah; because there is no doubt in these regarding their virtue and soundness; and the 'Straight Way' is the path of those on whom Allāh has bestowed His Grace, of the Prophets, the Siddīqūn (those followers of the Prophets who were first and foremost to believe in them), the martyrs, and the righteous; and how excellent these companions are!"

And from the most astounding of things is the fact that some "Shaykhs" have authored books on *Dhikr,* which contain innovated words of remembrance, and yet they named them *The Right Path—*

Subhānallāh! The Right Path is the one that the Messenger (ﷺ) was upon:

$$﴿ وَأَنَّ هَـٰذَا صِرَٰطِى مُسْتَقِيمًا فَٱتَّبِعُوهُ وَلَا تَتَّبِعُوا۟ ٱلسُّبُلَ فَتَفَرَّقَ بِكُمْ عَن سَبِيلِهِۦ ﴾$$

"And verily, this is my Straight Path, so follow it, and follow not (other) paths, for they will separate you away from His Path." [Sūrah al-An'ām (6):153]

What they should really be called is *The Crooked Path*; because the Right Path is the one that was taken by the Messenger of Allāh (ﷺ). Every path to Paradise is blocked except the path of the Noble Messenger (ﷺ).

On the authority of Abū Hurairah (رضي الله عنه) who reported that the Messenger of Allāh (ﷺ) said:

كل أمتي يدخلون الجنة إلا من أبى " . قيل: ومن يأبى يا رسول الله قال: " من أطاعني دخل الجنة، ومن عصاني فقد أبى

"Everyone from my *Ummah* (nation) will enter Paradise except those who refuse." He was asked: "Who will refuse?" He (ﷺ) said: "Whoever obeys me shall

enter Paradise, and whosoever disobeys me refuses to (enter Paradise)."[111]

3.   **Persistency in asking Allāh (عَزَّوَجَلَّ):** A person should not despair and give up [on his *Du'ā*] and say: "I supplicated and supplicated and it was not answered," rather, he should persist and constantly turn to his Master (تَبَارَكَوَتَعَالَى). And *Sūrah al-Fātihah* serves as evidence for highlighting the importance of being persistent in *Du'ā* since it is the Seven Oft-Repeated Verses that are to be read in every unit of *Salāh* by obligation whether in an obligatory or optional prayer; this affirms that being steadfast upon the Religion of Allāh is from the greatest required acts to be performed day and night. Thus, you repeatedly ask Allāh for guidance in the *Salāh*, in the *Du'ā* al-Qunūt and in the general supplications. So the Muslim should continuously persist in supplicating, asking and requesting from Allāh (تَبَارَكَوَتَعَالَى) per His statement:

$$ ﴿ ٱدْعُواْ رَبَّكُمْ تَضَرُّعًا وَخُفْيَةً ﴾ $$

"Invoke your Lord with humility and in secret." [Sūrah al-A'rāf (7):55]

One supplicates to Allah (جَلَّوَعَلَا), hoping that his request will be fulfilling or protecting him from an evil similar to it or storing it for him in the form of a reward on the Day of Resurrection.

---

[111] Reported by al-Bukhārī (7280)

4.   **Being Resolved in the *Du'ā* and Request:** The Messenger of Allāh (صَلَّ ٱللَّهُ عَلَيْهِ وَسَلَّمَ) said:

لَا يَقُولُ أَحَدُكُمُ اللَّهُمَّ اغْفِرْ لِي إِنْ شِئْتَ اللَّهُمَّ ارْحَمْنِي إِنْ شِئْتَ لِيَعْزِمِ الْمَسْأَلَةَ فَإِنَّهُ لاَ مُكْرِهَ لَ

"You must not supplicate: 'O Allāh, forgive me if You wish; O Allāh bestow mercy on me if You wish.' But beg Allāh with certitude for no one has the power to compel Allāh."[112]

What is required in the *Du'ā* is a firm conviction, so one must not be relaxed in his supplication and show weakness in his approach or certainty while invoking Allāh (تَبَارَكَ وَتَعَالَى). What we also find from the series of guidelines found in *Sūrah al-Fātihah* is that one should be resolved in his request for guidance and his hope in Allāh in granting him that while avoiding being lax and indifferent in his supplication.

5.   **Having a Conscious Heart:** A person's heart must be present when supplicating and not inattentive. The Prophet (عَلَيْهِ ٱلصَّلَاةُ وَٱلسَّلَامُ) said:

ادْعُوا اللَّهَ وَأَنْتُمْ مُوقِنُونَ بِالإِجَابَةِ وَاعْلَمُوا أَنَّ اللَّهَ لاَ يَسْتَجِيبُ دُعَاءً مِنْ قَلْبٍ غَافِلٍ لاَهٍ

---

[112] Reported by al-Bukhārī (6339) and Muslim (2679)

"Call upon Allāh while being certain of being answered, and know that Allāh does not respond to a supplication from the heart of one heedless and occupied by play."[113]

What is required from the supplicating person is to have a conscious heart and to turn full of hope to his Master (Allāh) while certain that He will answer his supplication; *Sūrah al-Fātihah* similarly address this in its preparing the supplicating person in the great introduction that precedes the *Du'ā*:

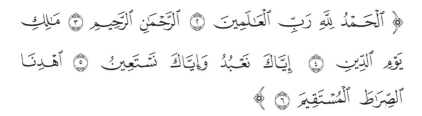

"All the praises and thanks are to Allāh, the Lord of the ʿĀlamīn (mankind, jinn and all that exists). The Most Gracious, the Most Merciful. The Only Owner (and the Only Ruling Judge) of the Day of Recompense (i.e., the Day of Resurrection). You (Alone) we worship, and You (Alone) we ask for help (for each and everything). (5) Guide us to the Straight Way." [Sūrah al-Fātihah (1): 1-6]

Allāh did not state this supplication right away:

---

[113] Reported by at-Tirmidhī (3479) and grade *Hasan* by al-Albānī (رحمه الله) in *Sahīh Sunan at-Tirmidhī* (3/434)

$$ ﴿ ٱهۡدِنَا ٱلصِّرَٰطَ ٱلۡمُسۡتَقِيمَ ٦ ﴾ $$

Guide us to the Straight Way. (*al-Fātihah*: 6)

But instead, Allāh (تَبَارَكَوَتَعَالَى) is mentioned, glorified, exalted and praised before the *Du'ā*; and this is a form of preparation for the heart so that it is fully turned to Allāh (تَبَارَكَوَتَعَالَى) when it invokes Him (عَزَّوَجَلَّ).

6.   Using Legislated Means to Seek Nearness to Allāh (تَبَارَكَوَتَعَالَى) (*at-Tawassul*): This is a vital yet dangerous subject, and many people err regarding it due to lack of understanding and lack of proper knowledge concerning the legislated *Tawassul* (means to seek nearness to Allāh). For this reason, the scholars said: "There is a legislated *Tawassul* and an impermissible *Tawassul*."

The Legislated *Tawassul*: It is three matters, and they are all mentioned in *Sūrah al-Fātihah*:

First matter: Seeking nearness to Allāh (تَبَارَكَوَتَعَالَى) through His Names and Attributes—and this is the highest form of *Tawassul*. Allāh (سُبۡحَانَهُوَتَعَالَى) said:

$$ ﴿ وَلِلَّهِ ٱلۡأَسۡمَآءُ ٱلۡحُسۡنَىٰ فَٱدۡعُوهُ بِهَآ ﴾ $$

"And (all) the Most Beautiful Names belong to Allāh, so call on Him by them." [Sūrah al-A'rāf (7):180]

And He (سُبْحَانَهُوَتَعَالَى) said

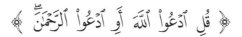

"Say (O Muḥammad صَلَّىاللهُعَلَيْهِوَسَلَّمَ**): "Invoke Allāh or invoke the Most Gracious (Allāh)." [Sūrah al-Isrā (17):110]**

And these two names of Allāh mentioned in *Sūrah al-Fātihah* before the *Du'ā* are a means to seek nearness to Allāh. Thus, *Tawassul* through the Names and Attributes of Allāh (تَبَارَكَوَتَعَالَى) is referred to in *Sūrah al-Fātihah*:

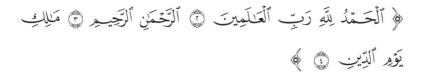

"All the praises and thanks are to Allāh, the Lord of the ʿĀlamīn (mankind, jinn and all that exists). The Most Gracious, the Most Merciful. The Only Owner (and the Only Ruling Judge) of the Day of Recompense (i.e., the Day of Resurrection)." [Sūrah al-Fātihah (1):2-4]

This is a great means to seek nearness to Allāh revealed in the *Qur'ān* and in the Sunnah of the Prophet (صَلَّىاللهُعَلَيْهِوَسَلَّمَ); it is specifically mentioned in *Sūrah al-Fātihah*.

Other matter: Seeking nearness to Allāh with your righteous deeds: With your worship and sincerity for Him, with your reliance and hope in Him, with your veneration and entrustment of Him with your affairs and with your humility before Him—this is a beneficial form of *Tawassul*:

﴾ رَبَّنَآ إِنَّنَا سَمِعْنَا مُنَادِيًا يُنَادِى لِلْإِيمَٰنِ أَنْ ءَامِنُواْ بِرَبِّكُمْ فَآمَنَّاۚ رَبَّنَا فَٱغْفِرْ لَنَا ذُنُوبَنَا ﴿

"Our Lord! Verily, we have heard the call of one (Muḥammad ﷺ) calling to Faith: 'Believe in your Lord,' and we have believed. Our Lord! Forgive us of our sins." [Sūrah Āli ʿImrān (3):193]

In this verse, 'Faith' is mentioned as a means of seeking nearness to Allāh (جَلَّوَعَلَا). Therefore, *Tawassul* can be through Faith, righteous deeds, *Tawḥīd* and loving the Messenger and following him (ﷺ); these are all righteous deeds through which nearness to Allāh (تَبَارَكَوَتَعَالَى) can be sought; this is found in *Sūrah al-Fātihah* in your statement before the *Duʿā*:

﴾ إِيَّاكَ نَعْبُدُ وَإِيَّاكَ نَسْتَعِينُ ۝ ﴿

"You (Alone) we worship, and You (Alone) we ask for help (for each and everything)." [Sūrah al-Fātihah (1):5]

Meaning, You Exclusively, O Allāh, I worship, and from You Exclusively, I seek assistance: Guide me to the Straight Path.

So now in *Sūrah al-Fātihah*, you have made *Tawassul* with two of its types: Through the Names and Attributes of Allāh and through your worship of Allāh (سُبْحَانَهُوَتَعَالَى).

Third matter: Seeking nearness to Allāh through the supplications of righteous, living and present people; for example, you ask a man in front of you, who you assume to be from the people of goodness and piety: "Supplicate to Allāh for me," or, "Supplicate for the Muslims," or what is similar to this—there is no problem in this. As for making *Tawassul* through people that are alive but not present in front of you as is the case with the people of misguidance; like a person requesting something from his Shaykh who is in another country, or making requests from people who have passed away and are cut off from fulfilling good deeds, this is not permissible. There is no evidence for this in the Book of Allāh or the Sunnah of His Prophet (ﷺ) proofing the legislation of what is similar to this act.

Then, *Tawassul* to Allāh can be made through His Names and Attributes, Faith, worship, and obedience of the servant to Allāh and through the supplications of righteous living people. This third type could also be extracted from His statement:

$$ \text{﴿ ۞ ٱهۡدِنَا ٱلصِّرَاطَ ٱلۡمُسۡتَقِيمَ ۞ ﴾} $$

"Guide us to the Straight Way." [Sūrah al-Fātihah (1):6]

Because with this *Du'ā*, you are supplicating for yourself and others; and the *Du'ā* of a Muslim for his Muslim brothers in their absence will be answered. And when the believer supplicates for his brother, Allāh entrusts an angel to say: "And may you get that as well." On the authority of Abū ad-Dardā' (ﷺ) who reported that the Prophet (ﷺ) said:

دَعْوَةُ الْمَرْءِ الْمُسْلِمِ لِأَخِيهِ بِظَهْرِ الْغَيْبِ مُسْتَجَابَةٌ عِنْدَ رَأْسِهِ مَلَكٌ مُوَكَّلٌ كُلَّمَا دَعَا لِأَخِيهِ بِخَيْرٍ قَالَ الْمَلَكُ الْمُوَكَّلُ بِهِ آمِينَ وَلَكَ بِمِثْلٍ

"The supplication of a Muslim for his (Muslim) brother in his absence will certainly be answered. Every time he makes a supplication for good for his brother, the angel appointed for this particular task says: 'Āmīn! May it be for you, too.'" [114]

Supplication for the believers in their absence has tremendous rewards that cannot be counted. The Messenger of Allāh (صَلَّى ٱللَّهُ عَلَيْهِ وَسَلَّمَ) said:

"Whoever seeks forgiveness for the believing men and women, Allāh will write for him a good deed for every believing man and women." [115]

So, when you say in your *Du'ā*:

اللَّهُمَّ اغْفِرْ لِلْمُسْلِمِينَ وَالْمُسْلِمَاتِ وَالْمُؤْمِنِينَ وَالْمُؤْمِنَاتِ الْأَحْيَاءِ مِنْهُمْ وَالْأَمْوَاتِ

---

[114] Reported by Muslim (2733)
[115] Reported by at-Tabarānī and graded *Hasan* by al-Albānī (رَحِمَهُ ٱللَّهُ) in *Sahīh al-Jāmi'* (6026)

"O Allāh, forgive the Muslim men and women and the believing men and women, the living and deceased from them,"

You will gain millions of good deeds by the Praise of Allāh; because you will earn a good deed for every Muslim, whether they are alive or dead, from the time of Adam to the time when Allāh will inherit the earth and whoever is upon it. Then is it befitting for you to restrict your supplications to yourself and forget your brothers? Allāh (سُبْحَانَهُوَتَعَالَى) said:

﴿ فَٱعْلَمْ أَنَّهُۥ لَآ إِلَٰهَ إِلَّا ٱللَّهُ وَٱسْتَغْفِرْ لِذَنۢبِكَ وَلِلْمُؤْمِنِينَ وَٱلْمُؤْمِنَٰتِ ﴾

"So, know (O Muḥammad ﷺ) that Lā ilāha ill-allāh (none has the right to be worshipped but Allāh), and ask forgiveness for your sin, and also for (the sin of) believing men and believing women." [Sūrah Muḥammad (47):19]

And He (سُبْحَانَهُوَتَعَالَى) said:

﴿ وَٱلَّذِينَ جَآءُو مِنۢ بَعْدِهِمْ يَقُولُونَ رَبَّنَا ٱغْفِرْ لَنَا وَلِإِخْوَٰنِنَا ٱلَّذِينَ سَبَقُونَا بِٱلْإِيمَٰنِ ﴾

**"And those who came after them say: "Our Lord! Forgive our brethren who have preceded us in Faith and us."
[Sūrah al-Ḥashr (59):10]**

On the authority of Abū Hurairah (رضي الله عنه) who said:

قَامَ رَسُولُ اللَّهِ صلى الله عليه وسلم فِي صَلاَةٍ وَقُمْنَا مَعَهُ، فَقَالَ أَعْرَابِيٌّ
وَهُوَ فِي الصَّلاَةِ اللَّهُمَّ ارْحَمْنِي وَمُحَمَّدًا، وَلاَ تَرْحَمْ مَعَنَا أَحَدًا. فَلَمَّا سَلَّمَ
النَّبِيُّ صلى الله عليه وسلم قَالَ لِلأَعْرَابِيِّ "لَقَدْ حَجَّرْتَ وَاسِعًا". يُرِيدُ
رَحْمَةَ اللَّهِ

"Allāh's Messenger (صَلَّى اللَّهُ عَلَيْهِ وَسَلَّمَ) stood up for the prayer, and we too stood up along with him. Then a Bedouin shouted while offering prayer. 'O Allāh! Bestow Your Mercy on Muḥammad and me only and do not bestow it on anybody else along with us.' When the Prophet (صَلَّى اللَّهُ عَلَيْهِ وَسَلَّمَ) had finished his prayer with the *Taslīm*, he said to the Bedouin, 'You have limited (narrowed) a very vast (thing),' meaning Allāh's Mercy."[116]

Hence, the Muslim asks Allāh (جَلَّ وَعَلَا) for His Mercy and Forgiveness for himself and his Muslim brothers—he includes them in his *Du'ā* just as he would love for them to include him in their supplications. So, these are the three legislated means of *Tawassul*.

---

[116] Reported by al-Bukhārī (6010)

2. The Impermissible *Tawassul:* This is everything outside of the three legislated means, and it could be classified as either *Shirk* (associating partners with Allāh in worship) or an innovation. As for the *Tawassul* that is *Shirk,* it could be in the form of supplicating to other than Allāh, like a person saying: "Grant me support O so and so," or, "Aid me O so and so," or, "I implore you for such and such O so and so;" this is all *Shirk* with Allāh even if its perpetrator calls it *Tawassul* as some of them might actually claim that such acts are a means to seek nearness to Allāh. And how can supplicating to other than Allāh be *Tawassul*? Yes, it is a *Tawassul,* one to falsehood:

﴿ وَلَقَدْ أُوحِيَ إِلَيْكَ وَإِلَى ٱلَّذِينَ مِن قَبْلِكَ لَئِنْ أَشْرَكْتَ لَيَحْبَطَنَّ عَمَلُكَ وَلَتَكُونَنَّ مِنَ ٱلْخَاسِرِينَ ۝ بَلِ ٱللَّهَ فَٱعْبُدْ وَكُن مِّنَ ٱلشَّاكِرِينَ ۝ ﴾

"And indeed it has been revealed to you (O Muḥammad ﷺ), as it was to those (Allāh's Messengers) before you: "If you join others in worship with Allāh, (then) surely (all) your deeds will be in vain, and you will certainly be among the losers." Nay! But worship Allāh (Alone and no one else) and be among the grateful." [Sūrah az-Zumar (39):65-66]

Naming something with other than its name does not change its reality, like their naming of *Shirk* '*Tawassul*' (a means to seek nearness to Allāh), or usury 'a benefit,' or alcohol 'a spiritual drink,' or bribery 'an honorable gesture.'

On this note, many Muslims ask the following question: "Is it permissible to say in our *Du'ā*: 'O Allāh, we ask you with the honor of Muḥammad (ﷺ) or the honor of Abū Bakr or 'Umar or 'Uthmān or 'Alī,' or something similar to this?"

The answer: Firstly, it is befitting to know that the honor of the Messenger (ﷺ) is considered great by Allāh—and no Muslim who knows the Messenger (عَلَيْهِ الصَّلَاةُ وَالسَّلَامُ) will doubt this—and Allāh (جَلَّ وَعَلَا) said concerning 'Īsā (عَلَيْهِ السَّلَامُ) that he was:

$$ ﴾ وَجِيهًا فِى ٱلدُّنْيَا وَٱلْأَخِرَةِ ﴿ $$

"...Held in honor in this world and in the Hereafter." [Sūrah Āli 'Imrān (3):45]

And He said concerning Mūsā (عَلَيْهِ السَّلَامُ):

$$ ﴾ وَكَانَ عِندَ ٱللَّهِ وَجِيهًا ۝ ﴿ $$

"...And he was honorable before Allāh." [Sūrah al-Ahzaab (32):69]

And the Prophet (عَلَيْهِ السَّلَامُ) is more virtuous than 'Īsā and Mūsā, rather, he is more virtuous than all the prophets; so his honor is the greatest honor with Allāh, and no one will doubt this—this is an affirmed well-known matter. However, the question remains: Is it permissible for us to use the honor of the Prophet (ﷺ) to seek nearness to Allāh?

The answer to this question is the following: Let us look, if the Sunnah directs to this act and proves it, then it can be done; and if it does not direct us to this or give us a proof for it, it cannot be done, because the matter is one that necessitates following and imitating the Sunnah of the Prophet (ﷺ). The people of knowledge have looked into the *Ahādīth* of the Prophet (ﷺ). They found that there is not a single authentic firm *Hadīth* from the Prophet (ﷺ) that contains a proof for the legislation of using his honor as *Tawassul*. Yes, there are Ahādīth concerning this, but they are not authentic, like the *Hadīth* that is propagated amongst the general laymen: "Make *Tawassul* (seek nearness to Allāh) through my honor, for indeed, my honor is great by Allāh." This is a *Hadīth* that has no basis whatsoever in being attributed to the Messenger of Allāh (ﷺ) as explained by the people of knowledge.

There are, however, authentic narrations used as evidence for the permissibility of making *Tawassul* through his honor. Still, they do not contain a clear reference to this.

7. **Supplicating with the Concise and Comprehensive** *Du'ā:* The Messenger (عَلَيْهِ ٱلصَّلَاةُ وَٱلسَّلَامُ) said:

بُعِثْتُ بِجَوَامِعِ الْكَلِمِ

"I have been sent with *Jawāmi'al-Kalim* (i.e., the shortest expression carrying the widest meanings)."[117]

And 'Āishah (رَضِيَٱللَّهُعَنْهَا) said:

كَانَ رَسُولُ اللَّهِ صلى الله عليه وسلم يَسْتَحِبُّ الْجَوَامِعَ مِنَ الدُّعَاءِ وَيَدَعُ مَا سِوَى ذَلِكَ

"The Messenger of Allāh (صَلَّىٱللَّهُعَلَيْهِوَسَلَّمَ) use to love the concise and comprehensive *Du'ā*, and he would leave off other than them."[118]

He used to supplicate with the concise *Du'ā*, and that is why all his supplications (صلوات الله وسلامه عليه) are concise and comprehensive.

Look at this encompassing *Du'ā* in *Sūrah al-Fātihah*:

﴿ ٱهْدِنَا ٱلصِّرَٰطَ ٱلْمُسْتَقِيمَ ٦ ﴾

"Guide us to the Straight Way." [Sūrah al-Fātihah (1):6], until the end of the *Du'ā*, it has encompassed all good in this world and the Hereafter.

Similarly, it is upon a person to make all his supplications comprehensive as the Prophet (عَلَيْهِٱلصَّلَاةُوَٱلسَّلَامُ) directed us. And

---

[117] Reported by al-Bukhārī (2977) and Muslim (523)
[118] Reported by Abū Dāwūd (1482) and authenticated by al-Albānī (رَحِمَهُٱللَّهُ) in *Sahīh Sunan Abī Dāwūd* (1/408)

whoever restricts himself to his (عَلَيْهِ الصَّلَاةُ وَالسَّلَامُ) invocations, he will indeed be supplicating with concise and comprehensive *Du'ā*. *He* will obtain the keys to all good and the completion of the affair in this world and the next.

And one should be cautious from transgressing in *Du'ā* by mentioning the intricate details that some of the people mention without any proof or guidance. On the authority of Ibn Sa'ad who said that: "My father heard while I was supplicating: 'O Allāh, I ask You for Paradise, its blessings, its beauty, its…, its…, and I seek Your refuge from the Hell and its iron chains and collars and..and…' So he said: 'O my son, verily, I heard the Messenger of Allāh (صَلَّى اللَّهُ عَلَيْهِ وَسَلَّمَ) saying:

'There will be people who will exceed the limits in supplication.' So, do not be from them. If you are granted Paradise, then you will be given Paradise and what it contains of good; and if you are protected from the Hell, then you will be granted safety from it and what it contains of evil.'"[119]

To Supplicate with Fear and Hope: To be both fearful and hopeful when supplicating. And a person should not lean too much to the side of hope or fear; because if he is more optimistic than afraid, he will feel safe from the plan of Allāh; and if one is more fearful than hopeful, he might despair in the mercy of Allāh, as Allāh said:

---

[119] Reported by Abū Dāwūd (1480) and authenticated by al-Albānī (رَحِمَهُ اللَّهُ) in *Sahīh Sunan Abī Dāwūd* (1/407)

﴾ إِنَّهُمْ كَانُوا يُسَارِعُونَ فِي الْخَيْرَاتِ وَيَدْعُونَنَا رَغَبًا وَرَهَبًا وَكَانُوا لَنَا خَاشِعِينَ ۝ ﴿

"Verily, they used to hasten on to do good deeds, and they used to call on Us with hope and fear, and used to humble themselves before Us." [Sūrah al-Anbiyā (21):90]

﴾ ادْعُوا رَبَّكُمْ تَضَرُّعًا وَخُفْيَةً إِنَّهُ لَا يُحِبُّ الْمُعْتَدِينَ ۝ وَلَا تُفْسِدُوا فِي الْأَرْضِ بَعْدَ إِصْلَاحِهَا وَادْعُوهُ خَوْفًا وَطَمَعًا إِنَّ رَحْمَتَ اللَّهِ قَرِيبٌ مِنَ الْمُحْسِنِينَ ۝ ﴿

"Invoke your Lord with humility and in secret. He likes not the aggressors. And do not make mischief on the earth, after it has been set in order, and invoke Him with fear and hope; Surely, Allāh's Mercy is (ever) near unto the good-doers." [Sūrah al-A'rāf (7):55-56]

And this matter is mentioned in *Sūrah al-Fātihah*:

﴾ الرَّحْمَٰنِ الرَّحِيمِ ۝ مَالِكِ يَوْمِ الدِّينِ ۝ ﴿

"The Most Gracious, the Most Merciful. The Only Owner (and the Only Ruling Judge) of the Day of Recompense (i.e., the Day of Resurrection)." [Sūrah al-Fātihah (1):3-4]

When you read this while pondering and reflecting over Allāh's address, fear and hope will appear in your heart: hope for His Mercy and fear from His Punishment.

8.   **Being in a State of Purity:** The one supplicating should be in a state of purity. This is not a condition, but it is more complete. And if he is pure and in a *Salāh*, this is even more complete, and it is likely to be answered; and this is likewise referred to in *Sūrah al-Fātihah*, especially if the Muslim reads it in his *Salāh*—he will be privately addressing his Lord (تَبَارَكَوَتَعَالَى).

9.   **Repenting Before the *Du'ā*:** A repentance and seeking of forgiveness should antecede the supplication, and this can be found in some of the opening invocations for the *Salāh* that precede *al-Fātihah*:

اللَّهُمَّ بَاعِدْ بَيْنِي وَبَيْنَ خَطَايَاىَ كَمَا بَاعَدْتَ بَيْنَ الْمَشْرِقِ وَالْمَغْرِبِ، اللَّهُمَّ نَقِّنِي مِنَ الْخَطَايَا كَمَا يُنَقَّى الثَّوْبُ الأَبْيَضُ مِنَ الدَّنَسِ، اللَّهُمَّ اغْسِلْ خَطَايَاىَ بِالْمَاءِ وَالثَّلْجِ وَالْبَرَدِ

"O Allāh! Set me apart from my sins (faults) as the East and West are set apart from each other and clean me from sins as a white garment is cleaned of dirt (after thorough

washing). O Allāh, wash off my sins with water, snow, and hail."[120]

These are some matters tied to *Du'ā* that are referenced by this wonderful *Sūrah*. And it is upon every Muslim to know the value of *Du'ā*, its exalted status with Allāh (عَزَّوَجَلَّ), the servant's desperate need of it in all his situations and that *Du'ā* is the key to all good in this world and the Hereafter. It is also upon him to know the etiquettes and conditions of *Du'ā* as well as the specific times and places in which supplications are answered mentioned by the Sunnah such as the field of 'Arafah, the tops of mount *Safā* and *Marwah* and after throwing the pebbles at the *Jamarāt* (a ritual of *Hajj*) after the first and second *Jamrah* on the days of *Tashrīq* (the 11ᵗʰ, 12ᵗʰ and 13ᵗʰ day of Dhul Hijjah). And some specific times in which supplications are more likely to be accepted are *Laylatul-Qadr* (one of the last ten nights of *Ramadān*), the 'hour' on the day of *Jumu'ah* (Friday), the last third of the night and when in prostration. A person should seek these times and places in which supplications are answered, and these occasions must be within the limits of what has been legislated in the Sunnah of the Prophet (صَلَّىٱللَّهُعَلَيْهِوَسَلَّمَ).

Some of the people of knowledge combined the etiquettes and conditions of an accepted *Du'ā* in some elegant lines of poetry:

"They said that the conditions of an answered *Du'ā* are ten; announce this good news of success to the supplicating one: being pure and in prayer along with regret, a time of

---

focus and concentration, thinking positively [of Allāh] O conscious one, and nourishment from lawful sustenance, as well as not supplicating for a sin; and invoking [Allāh] with an appropriate Name while also being persistent."

As for the composer's statement: "announce this good news of success to the supplicating one," this means, give the glad tidings to him of success. An answered *Du'ā* if he adheres to the following [conditions] in his supplication:

❖   "Being pure and in prayer along with regret," meaning that he should be in a state of purity and in *Salāh*; this is not one of the conditions, but it is from the etiquettes and those things that complete the *Du'ā*.

❖   "A time of focus and concentration, thinking positively [of Allāh]," meaning, the supplication should be made in a virtuous time, and he should be focused in his *Du'ā* and fearful and repenting to Allāh; and that he should have good thoughts about Allāh, as Allāh (عَزَّوَجَلَّ) has said in the *Hadīth Qudsī*:

أَنَا عِنْدَ ظَنِّ عَبْدِي، فَلْيَظُنّ بِي مَا شَاءَ

'I am to my slave as he thinks of Me (i.e., I can do for him what he expects from Me), so let him think of Me what he wishes.'"121

❖   "And nourishment from lawful sustenance." This is also from the conditions that are referenced to in the poetry. It means that a person's food should pure and lawful; and this has been reported in the *Hadīth* of Abū Hurairah:

إِنَّ اللهَ طَيِّبٌ لَا يَقْبَلُ إِلَّا طَيِّبًا، وَإِنَّ اللهَ أَمَرَ الْمُؤْمِنِينَ بِمَا أَمَرَ بِهِ الْمُرْسَلِينَ فَقَالَ تَعَالَى: "يَا أَيُّهَا الرُّسُلُ كُلُوا مِنَ الطَّيِّبَاتِ وَاعْمَلُوا صَالِحًا"، وَقَالَ تَعَالَى: "يَا أَيُّهَا الَّذِينَ آمَنُوا كُلُوا مِنْ طَيِّبَاتِ مَا رَزَقْنَاكُمْ" ثُمَّ ذَكَرَ الرَّجُلَ يُطِيلُ السَّفَرَ أَشْعَثَ أَغْبَرَ يَمُدُّ يَدَيْهِ إِلَى السَّمَاءِ: يَا رَبِّ! يَا رَبِّ! وَمَطْعَمُهُ حَرَامٌ، وَمَشْرَبُهُ حَرَامٌ، وَمَلْبَسُهُ حَرَامٌ، وَغُذِّيَ بِالْحَرَامِ، فَأَنَّى يُسْتَجَابُ لَهُ؟

"The Prophet (ﷺ) said: 'Allāh is Good and accepts only that which is good.' Then he (ﷺ) mentioned [the case] of a man who, having journeyed far, is disheveled and dusty, and who spreads out his hands to the sky saying, 'O Lord! O Lord!' while his food is *Harām*

---

121 Reported by Ahmad (3/491) and authenticated by al-Albānī (رحمه الله) in *Sahīh al-Jāmi'* (4316)

(unlawful), his drink is *Harām*, his clothing is *Harām*, and he has been nourished with *Harām*, so how can [his supplication] be answered?'"[122]

❖   "As well as not supplicating for a sin," meaning that it is not permissible for a person to supplicate for a sin as has been affirmed from the Prophet (ﷺ):

لَا يَزَالُ يُسْتَجَابُ لِلْعَبْدِ مَا لَمْ يَدْعُ بِإِثْمٍ أَوْ قَطِيعَةِ رَحِمٍ مَا لَمْ يَسْتَعْجِلْ

"The supplication of the servant is granted so long as he does not supplicate for sin or for severing the ties of blood, or he does not become impatient."[123]

❖   "Invoking [Allāh] with an appropriate Name." He should choose from the Names of Allāh (تَبَارَكَوَتَعَالَى), which agrees with his request, and if he does not select an appropriate name, this will cause disharmony in his speech. Consequently, we find supplications coupled with proper names in the texts:

﴿ رَبَّنَا ٱفْتَحْ بَيْنَنَا وَبَيْنَ قَوْمِنَا بِٱلْحَقِّ وَأَنتَ خَيْرُ ٱلْفَٰتِحِينَ ۝ ﴾

---

[122] Reported by Muslim (1015)
[123] Reported by Muslim (92), (2735)

"Our Lord! Judge between our people in truth and us, for You are the Best of those who give judgment." [Sūrah al-A'rāf (7):89]

You should say:

رَبِّ اغْفِرْ لِي إِنَّكَ الْغَفُورُ الرَّحِيمُ

"O Allāh forgive me, for indeed, You are the Oft-Forgiving, the Bestower of Mercy."

So it should be like this, but if you invoke Allāh with a Name of His that does not match your request, then there be in an inconsistency, like a person saying: "O Allāh, bestow Your Mercy on me and forgive me, O One Who is severe in punishment;" this is not appropriate, what is befitting for him to say instead is: "O One Who is Oft-Forgiving, Most Merciful, O One Whose Mercy encompasses everything..." He should mention from Allāh's Beautiful Names what suits his request. Thus, the scholars cite a principle: "Every verse in the Noble *Qur'ān* that ends with a Name or Attribute of Allāh, the meanings contained in it must match this Name or Attribute mentioned at its conclusion."

It is narrated that a Bedouin once heard a man reciting the Statement of Allāh (سُبْحَانَهُوَتَعَالَى):

﴿ وَٱلسَّارِقُ وَٱلسَّارِقَةُ فَٱقْطَعُوٓاْ أَيْدِيَهُمَا جَزَآءً بِمَا كَسَبَا نَكَٰلًا مِّنَ ٱللَّهِ وَٱللَّهُ عَزِيزٌ حَكِيمٌ ﴿٣٨﴾ ﴾

"And (as for) the male thief and the female thief, cut off (from the wrist joint) their (right) hands as a recompense for that which they committed, a punishment by way of example from Allāh. And Allāh is All-Powerful, All-Wise." [Sūrah al-Mā'idah (5):38]

The man-made a mistake in the recitation, and he concluded the verse instead with: **"And Allāh the Oft-Forgiving, Most Merciful."** The Bedouin said: "This is not from the Speech of Allāh." The other man became angry and asked: "Do you deny the Speech of Allāh?" He said: "I do not deny it, but this is not from Allāh's Speech;" he found that the ending of the verse does not suit the cutting of the hand, the recompense, and the punishment. The man that was reciting then realized his mistake, and he corrected himself and read:

﴿ وَٱلسَّارِقُ وَٱلسَّارِقَةُ فَٱقۡطَعُوٓاْ أَيۡدِيَهُمَا جَزَآءَۢ بِمَا كَسَبَا نَكَٰلٗا مِّنَ ٱللَّهِۗ وَٱللَّهُ عَزِيزٌ حَكِيمٞ ٣٨ ﴾

And (as for) the male thief and the female thief, cut off (from the wrist joint) their (right) hands as a recompense for that which they committed, a punishment by way of example from Allāh. And Allāh is All-Powerful, All-Wise. (al-Mā'idah: 38)

The Bedouin thereupon said: "Yes! [Allāh is] All-Powerful and thus Just, and All-Wise and thus [he ruled for] the cutting." He is basically saying that the whole speech is now harmonious. This is why Ibn al-Qayyim (رحمة الله عليه) related this story in his book, *Jalā al-Afhām*; he said: "Surely when a person supplicates with a name that does not fit [his request], there will be an inconsistency in the speech."

❖   The poet then said: "While also being persistent," i.e., you should be unrelenting in asking Allāh (تَبَارَكَوَتَعَالَ), and you should invoke Him abundantly. Be constant in your request and knocking of the door; it is on the verge of being opened for you.

I ask Allāh (جَلَّوَعَلَا) with His Beautiful Names and Lofty Attributes to grant us *Tawfīq* and guide us to the Right Way.

9ᵀᴴ GUIDELINE: LOVE, HOPE, & FEAR

From the directives of this *Sūrah* is its reference to the pillars for the worship of the heart: Love, hope and fear, Allāh (سُبْحَانَهُ وَتَعَالَى) said:

﴿ أُوْلَٰٓئِكَ ٱلَّذِينَ يَدْعُونَ يَبْتَغُونَ إِلَىٰ رَبِّهِمُ ٱلْوَسِيلَةَ أَيُّهُمْ أَقْرَبُ وَيَرْجُونَ رَحْمَتَهُۥ وَيَخَافُونَ عَذَابَهُۥٓ إِنَّ عَذَابَ رَبِّكَ كَانَ مَحْذُورًا ۝ ﴾

"Those whom they call upon [like 'Īsā (Jesus) son of Maryam (Mary), 'Uzair (Ezra), angel] desire (for themselves) means of access to their Lord (Allāh), as to which of them should be the nearest and they ['Īsā (Jesus), 'Uzair (Ezra), angels and others] hope for His Mercy and fear His Torment. Verily, the Torment of your Lord is (something) to be afraid of!" [Sūrah al-Isrā (17):57]

It is a must that every act of worship be firmly established upon these three pillars of the heart: Love, hope, and fear. Thus, the Muslim offers *Salāh* because he loves Allāh, hopes for his rewards, and fears his punishment. It is for this reason that Talq Ibn Ḥabīb (رَحِمَهُ ٱللَّهُ) defined the *Taqwā* of Allāh as, "being obedient to Allāh upon a light from Allāh, hoping for His reward, leaving off disobedience to Him upon a light from Him and fearing His punishment."

And it is not permissible to worship Allāh with only love and no fear or hope; or with only fear and no love or hope; or with only hope and no fear or love—this is all false, as the one of the *Salaf* said:

> "The one who worships Allāh with only love is a *Zindīq*; the one who worships Allāh with only hope is a *Murji'* (a deviated sect that depends only on their belief in Allāh and desists from fulfilling good deeds); the one who worships Allāh with only fear is a *Kharijite*; but the one who worships Allāh with love, hope, and fear, he is a *Muwahhid* believer (one who singles out Allāh in his *Tawhīd*)."

So, you must worship Allāh with love, hope, and fear. Worship Him out of love for Him and while hoping for His rewards and fearing His punishment; these three pillars combined are mentioned in *Sūrah al-Fātihah*:

The first pillar is Love: It is in His Statement:

> "All the praises and thanks are for Allāh, the Lord of the *'Ālamīn* (mankind, jinn and all that exists)." [Sūrah al-Fātihah (1):2]

And the word '*al-Hamdu*,' it means all praise and exaltation is for Allāh with love—so praise with love is referred to as '*Hamd*.' And the particle '*al*' in '*al-Hamdu*,' it is used to denote all-inclusiveness, meaning that Allāh is deserving of all the praises and thanks: praise for His Blessings and praise for His Names and Attributes (سُبْحَانَهُوَتَعَالَى). Thus, this verse contains a proof for the first pillar, love:

﴿ ٱلْحَمْدُ لِلَّهِ رَبِّ ٱلْعَٰلَمِينَ ۝ ﴾

"All the praises and thanks are for Allāh, the Lord of the 'Ālamīn (mankind, jinn and all that exists)." [Sūrah al-Fātihah (1):2]

<u>The second pillar is Hope:</u> It is in His Statement:

﴿ ٱلرَّحْمَٰنِ ٱلرَّحِيمِ ۝ ﴾

"The Most Gracious, the Most Merciful." [Sūrah al-Fātihah (1):3]

If the servant carefully reads these two magnificent Names and contemplates over them and understands what they refer to in affirming the Mercy of Allāh (جَلَّوَعَلَا), there will form in his heart longing for Allāh's Mercy, as Allāh (سُبْحَانَهُوَتَعَالَى) said:

"They hope for His Mercy." [Sūrah al-Isrā (17):57]

<u>The third pillar is Fear:</u> It is in His Statement:

﴿ مَٰلِكِ يَوْمِ ٱلدِّينِ ۝ ﴾

"The Only Owner (and the Only Ruling Judge) of the Day of Recompense (i.e., the Day of Resurrection)." [Sūrah al-Fātihah (1):4]

When a person reading this brings to mind the Reckoning before Allāh [on the Day of Judgment], fear will come to his heart, but he will remain hopeful of Allāh's pardoning:

$$ \text{﴿ لِيَجْزِيَ ٱلَّذِينَ أَسَٰٓـُٔوا۟ بِمَا عَمِلُوا۟ وَيَجْزِيَ ٱلَّذِينَ أَحْسَنُوا۟ بِٱلْحُسْنَىٰ ۝ ﴾} $$

"…That He may requite those who do evil with that which they have done (i.e., punish them in Hell) and reward those who do good, with what is best (i.e., Paradise)." [Sūrah an-Najm (53):31]

And the terror of the situation of the Day of Resurrection is indeed great:

$$ \text{﴿ وَمَآ أَدْرَىٰكَ مَا يَوْمُ ٱلدِّينِ ۝ ثُمَّ مَآ أَدْرَىٰكَ مَا يَوْمُ ٱلدِّينِ ۝ يَوْمَ لَا تَمْلِكُ نَفْسٌ لِّنَفْسٍ شَيْـًٔا ۖ وَٱلْأَمْرُ يَوْمَئِذٍ لِّلَّهِ ۝ ﴾} $$

"And what will make you know what the Day of Recompense is? Again, what will make you know what the Day of Recompense is? (It will be) the Day when no person shall have power (to do) anything for another, and the Decision, that Day, will be (wholly) with Allāh." [Sūrah al-Infitār (82):17-19]

After this, the verse that follows [in *Sūrah al-Fātihah*] is:

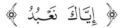

"You (Alone) we worship." [Sūrah al-Fātihah (1):5]

It is as if you are saying: "You Alone we worship O Allāh with the love that is referenced in:

$$﴾ ٱلۡحَمۡدُ لِلَّهِ رَبِّ ٱلۡعَٰلَمِينَ ۝ ﴿$$

"All the praises and thanks are for Allāh, the Lord of the *'Ālamīn*." [Sūrah al-Fātihah (1):2],

and with the hope that is referenced in:

"The Most Gracious, the Most Merciful" [Sūrah al-Fātihah (1):3],

and with the fear that is referenced in:

$$﴾ مَٰلِكِ يَوۡمِ ٱلدِّينِ ۝ ﴿$$

"The Only Owner (and the Only Ruling Judge) of the Day of Recompense (i.e., the Day of Resurrection)" [Sūrah al-Fātihah (1):4].

When these foundations of worship are fixed firmly, servitude will follow. After this, how can it be permitted for a person to say: "I am a servant of Allāh in love to Him only; I do not desire rewards, and I do not fear any punishment?" There is no doubt that this is complete nonsense. Ibrāhīm, the close friend of Allāh, the leader of the sincere monotheistic worshipers of Allāh, said:

$$﴿ وَٱجْعَلْنِي مِن وَرَثَةِ جَنَّةِ ٱلنَّعِيمِ ۝ ﴾$$

"And make me one of the inheritors of the Paradise of Delight." [Sūrah ash-Shu'arā (1):85]

And the Prophet (ﷺ) said to a man:

كَيْفَ تَقُولُ فِي الصَّلَاةِ " . قَالَ أَتَشَهَّدُ وَأَقُولُ اللَّهُمَّ إِنِّي أَسْأَلُكَ الْجَنَّةَ وَأَعُوذُ بِكَ مِنَ النَّارِ أَمَا إِنِّي لاَ أُحْسِنُ دَنْدَنَتَكَ وَلاَ دَنْدَنَةَ مُعَاذٍ . فَقَالَ النَّبِيُّ صلى الله عليه وسلم " حَوْلَهَا نُدَنْدِنُ

"What do you say in prayer?" He replied: "I first recite _Tashahhud_ (supplication recited in sitting position), and then I say: O Allāh, I ask You for Paradise, and I seek refuge in You from Hell-Fire, but I do not understand your murmuring and the murmuring of Mu'ādh (what you or he says in the prayer)." The Prophet (ﷺ) said: Our murmuring resolves around the same thing (supplicating for Paradise and seeking refuge from Hell-fire)."[124]

---

[124] Reported by Abū Dāwūd (792) and authenticated by al-Albānī (رَحِمَهُ اللَّهُ) in _Sahīh Sunan Abī Dāwūd_ (1/225)

And the *Du'ā* he (عَلَيْهِٱلصَّلَاةُوَٱلسَّلَامُ) used to make most was:

رَبَّنَا آتِنَا فِي اَلدُّنْيَا حَسَنَةً, وَفِي اَلْآخِرَةِ حَسَنَةً, وَقِنَا عَذَابَ اَلنَّارِ

"O our Lord, grants us the best in this life and the best in the next life, and protect us from the punishment of the Fire."[125]

Some of them are even worse in their misguidance, they say: "Worshipping Allāh out of hope in gaining his reward or fear of his punishment, this is the worship of the businessmen;" this is undoubtedly from clear misguidance and refuge is sought with Allāh. In fact, all the prophets encouraged the people to long for Paradise and warned them from Hell-Fire. They themselves asked Allāh for Paradise and sought protection from Him from the Hell-Fire. So if a person comes and says: "I do not desire Paradise or fear the Fire, rather, I only want to worship Allāh with love;" know that he is astray and deviated from the Straight Path of Allāh, from His Straight Religion and from adherence to the way of the Prophets and Messengers.

On the authority of 'Āishah (رَضِيَٱللَّهُعَنْهَا) who said that the Messenger of Allāh (صَلَّىٱللَّهُعَلَيْهِوَسَلَّمَ) taught her this *Du'ā*:

---

[125] Reported by al-Bukhārī (6389) and Muslim (2690)

اللَّهُمَّ إِنِّي أَسْأَلُكَ مِنَ الْخَيْرِ كُلِّهِ عَاجِلِهِ وَآجِلِهِ مَا عَلِمْتُ مِنْهُ وَمَا لَمْ أَعْلَمْ

وَأَعُوذُ بِكَ مِنَ الشَّرِّ كُلِّهِ عَاجِلِهِ وَآجِلِهِ مَا عَلِمْتُ مِنْهُ وَمَا لَمْ أَعْلَمْ اللَّهُمَّ

إِنِّي أَسْأَلُكَ مِنْ خَيْرِ مَا سَأَلَكَ عَبْدُكَ وَنَبِيُّكَ وَأَعُوذُ بِكَ مِنْ شَرِّ مَا عَاذَ

بِهِ عَبْدُكَ وَنَبِيُّكَ اللَّهُمَّ إِنِّي أَسْأَلُكَ الْجَنَّةَ وَمَا قَرَّبَ إِلَيْهَا مِنْ قَوْلٍ أَوْ عَمَلٍ

وَأَعُوذُ بِكَ مِنَ النَّارِ وَمَا قَرَّبَ إِلَيْهَا مِنْ قَوْلٍ أَوْ عَمَلٍ وَأَسْأَلُكَ أَنْ تَجْعَلَ

كُلَّ قَضَاءٍ قَضَيْتَهُ لِي خَيْرًا

"O Allāh, I ask You for all that is good, in this world and in the Hereafter, what I know and what I am unaware of. O Allāh, I seek refuge with You from all evil, in this world and in the Hereafter, what I know and what I do not know of it. O Allāh, I ask You for the good that Your slave and Prophet has asked You for, and I seek refuge with You from the evil from which Your slave and Prophet sought refuge. O Allāh, I ask You for Paradise and for that which brings one closer to it, in word and deed, and I seek refuge in You from Hell and from that which brings one closer to it, in word and deed. And I ask You to make every decree that You decree for me good."[126]

---

[126] Reported by Ibn Mājah (3846) and authenticated by al-Albānī (رَحِمَهُ ٱللَّهُ) in *Sahīh Sunan Ibn Mājah* (3116)

It has been reported abundantly in the supplications of the Prophet (ﷺ) that he would ask Allāh for Paradise, seek His protection from the Fire and the punishment of the grave and seek His refuge from His punishment; then these people that negate come and say: "We do not want Paradise or fear the Fire, we only love Allāh?!" This is misguidance and deviance; it is upon you to worship Allāh out of love for Him (تَبَارَكَوَتَعَالَى), hope in His bounties, and fear of His punishment. This is why—as has preceded—the scholars (رَحِمَهُمُاللَّه) affirm that: "Indeed, all types of worship must have three pillars and they must be present in the heart: Love of Allāh, hope of His rewards and fear of His punishment."

In conclusion, it is a must that a person fears Allāh and knows His religion, the Straight Path, and the Upright Way. He should turn to the Religion of Allāh (جَلَّوَعَلَا) rightly: Loving Allāh (تَبَارَكَوَتَعَالَى), longing for His Mercy, and fearing His punishment.

I ask Allāh, the Most Generous with His Beautiful Names and Lofty Attributes, to make all of us firm on His Straight Path. O Allāh, guide us to the Straight Way:

﴿ صِرَاطَ ٱلَّذِينَ أَنْعَمْتَ عَلَيْهِمْ غَيْرِ ٱلْمَغْضُوبِ عَلَيْهِمْ وَلَا ٱلضَّآلِّينَ ۝ ﴾

"The Way of those on whom You have bestowed Your Grace, not (the way) of those who earned Your Anger (such as the Jews), nor of those who went astray (such as the Christians)."

O Allāh, rectify our religion for us, which is the safeguard of our affairs; and rectify our worldly (matters), wherein is our livelihood; make right our afterlife to which is our return; make our life (a means of) an increase in every good and make death (for us) as a rest from every evil. O Allāh, forgive us for all our sins, the small and the great, the first and the last, the open and the secret. O Allāh, forgive us and our parents, and the Muslim men and women, and the believing men and women, the living from them and the dead. O Allāh, we ask you for that which incites Your Mercy and the means of Your forgiveness, the benefit from every good deed, safety from every sin, success in attaining Paradise and deliverance from Fire.

And the close of our request is: All the praises and thanks are to Allāh, the Lord of all that exists, and may Allāh raise the rank of our Prophet, Muḥammad and send peace upon him and all his family and companions.

Printed in Great Britain
by Amazon